Halfway Home

Collected Poems

Marlaina Donato

Ekstasis Multimedia
Blairstown, New Jersey

Halfway Home/Marlaina Donato
Blairstown, New Jersey: Ekstasis Multimedia, LLC, 2014
Ekstasis Multimedia: www.booksandbrush.net

ISBN-13: 978-0692359761
ISBN-10: 0692359761

Photography and design: Marlaina Donato

Contents

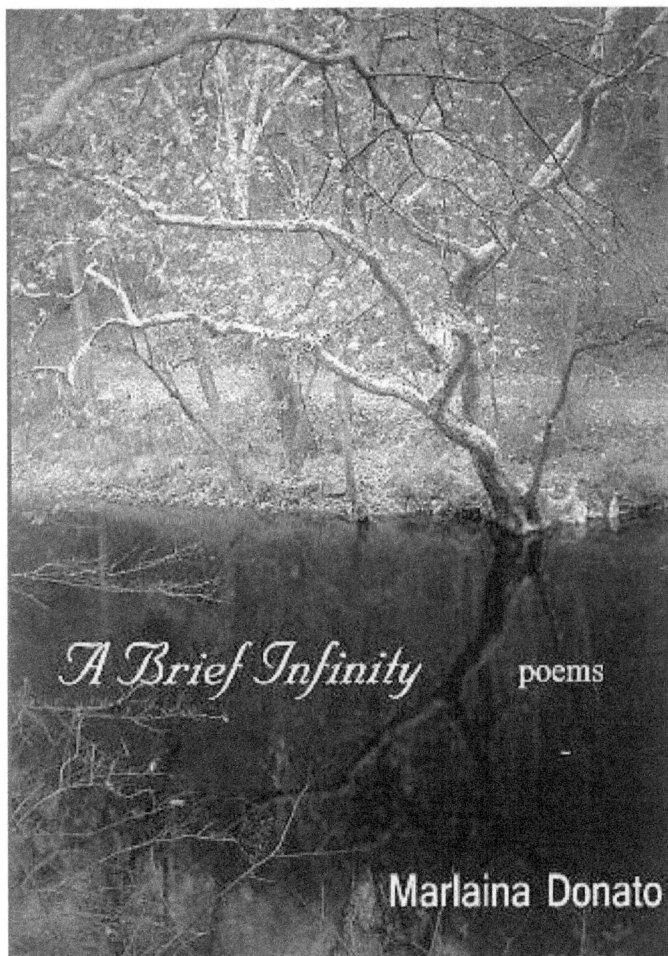

A Brief Infinity   poems

Marlaina Donato

A Brief Infinity

Beauty's Chord

Genesis

Morning white, new snow

Canvas

Paper

Slipping along the stark incline of possibility

Boots hesitate to violate a virgin meadow

The brush pauses before plunging into naked grain

The pen trembles with words

The heart lingers between beats

In a tundra of ember

Fearing the wasteland

Of stillborn could-have-beens

White morning, new snow

Canvas

Paper

Purity of pain that urges us to begin

More difficult than the middle or The End

"Begin," the New whispers, "Begin."

Autumn

After the fields are combed and the orchards are bare,

Autumn tarries with tears in her eyes.

She stains the forests with her auburn hair

And blows out the fire flies.

Her hands ache from harvest labor, and she longs for sleep.

Adorned in the amber of October fires,

She waits until November to weep

And sings in the cricket choirs.

Only the melancholy glimpse her face

As she weaves misty scarves through the maple's drowsy eaves.

She cools the nights, but warm is her embrace.

Then with one last leap of strength, she takes the leaves.

Ambrosia

Drink from the deep, my Soul,

And taste the silver of its surface.

Thirsty Soul, out of density, destiny,

Fly!

Drink the nectar of the night;

Touch the blue flame of the winds, heaven's pulse.

Dissolve into the dawn, singing crystal.

Shimmering Self, into the universes within,

Fly!

Fly the speed of stillness.

Let your heart be a bow against Beauty's chord.

Drink from the deep, my Soul,

Drink the deep and the silver of its surface.

Fly!

Fly the speed of stillness.

A Year

Morning is dappled with memories

Of that year when we lived

Amid shivering oak trees

In a house with a red door;

The year you taught me how to make a fire,

And I felt more accomplished

Than if I had saved a drowning world;

The year mornings were jarred by the banter of ravens,

And we drank spiced cocoa and plotted the future.

It was the year I cried myself to sleep,

And you prayed that we would live;

The year we huddled against circumstance

And clung to the hope of spring.

As the years descend like early snow,

That year lives within me,

The year we lived amid shivering oak trees

In a house with a red door.

Twenty-Something

She is the serpent's sister

With denim hips reciting the names of many lovers

She moves with the ease of blowing sands

As she shifts against the half-open door

Inhaling admiration from her latest cigarette

Exhaling alibis into the indifferent air

What illusion of wisdom in her beauty

As I sit here knowing better

Knowing bitter

The young envying the young

Resolution

This life

Striving to be an ocean...

Immense

Constant

Unbroken

This life

Striving to be a forest...

Wild

Fruitful

Resourceful

Let this life

Be what it is- a desert, a barren womb

Until unexpected rain

A brief infinity of flowers

Beauty out of nothingness

Then back into nothingness

Never repeated

Magma

A red leaf stains the wind, a drop of summer's blood.

While there is still time,

While there is still singing in the fields,

Listen

To the sonnet bound inside my fist,

The scream your eyes forge in me.

Before the veins of youth shrivel under snow,

Listen

While I sing your thorns back to you,

Sing the gold pain of your breath,

Sing the magma inside the steel.

Listen...

It is yours, this blood song.

Wounds

Refugees of the internal war,

We seek shelter here tonight.

Our souls are shattered flames

While the stars remain indifferent.

Wisdom is a bitter cup,

And we have drunk until sickness.

We love until pain

And ecstasy again

Explodes in the blood.

How our wounds find each other,

Open and too deep for resolution;

Love, too fragile for our rage

Can only live an hour.

Dark Wind

New Boots

Walking down the street, rhythm of heels

Feeling dangerous

And bold as a Chihuahua

Barking at a St. Bernard

From behind a fence

Love's Labor

Across a bed wet with sun, we love in the light.

Our bodies praying fire, we ride the day

Until I rest my ear against your heart

And shadows descend like gray birds across your skin.

We have loved well this day,

Labored well in Beauty's house.

We have loved well this day,

This day in forever.

Ascent

Plucked from the bosom of ideals, he meets death alone

Beneath the stars.

On scorching soil, all is forgotten-

Enemy

Cause

Strategy;

All is eclipsed

In a single thought- that of the blond-haired son

Who has his father's eyes.

An eon of minutes

And then sudden flight

Into infinity;

As blazing and focused as a flare into darkness,

A soul ascends

Through smoke,

Over fire.

Home.

Dew

There is neither smile nor twin face

Upon which to press my cheek to your memory;

No voice among man, bird, or wind

That can harmonize with my remembrance.

Upon which dream have you embarked?

Tell me...so my sleeping heart may wake

To find your eyes again

Somewhere on Death's stormless course

On the night-blackened deep.

Upon which sunbeam to you skip barefoot?

Tell me...so these shackles of sorrow

May unfold wings drunk with light.

Within which flower do you leave a kiss?

Tell me...so I may drink the dew there and quench my life.

A Garden

White iris, the brides of the garden,

Toss veils of shadow against the wall.

Our hands wrist-deep in soil,

Whisper promises of roots and flowers

While the tulips flare their Gypsy skirts,

And the fountain sings in a language

Only the lilies know.

Winters from now,

I will take these out of my bag of memories

And shake off the years

To taste dappled days scented with cedar.

And flowers, well-versed in their mother's origins,

Will tell stories about ladies wrist-deep in soil

Who had faith in seeds.

Liturgy

After a long day's rain,

The night is awash with spirits.

Twilight is a sapphire

Faceted by the hands of Deity.

Tree, grass, wanderer...

And all that have longed reach heavenward.

Stillness is sovereign

In the Liturgy of Hours;

And the soul, splintered and scattered,

Gathers unto itself again.

Nomad

My hands travel your night sands;

You shiver in the dark wind of my longing,

Lover of cinnamon and amber,

Lover of a thousand deserts

My soul has traveled.

Sing your hunger in tones of lapis;

Dance the dawn between my thighs.

Shake the centuries from your hair

And teach me the language of sudden rain

On the thousand deserts

My soul has traveled.

Solstice

Calligraphy of branches

Etched on the morning's snowy paper

Raven landing

Punctuation

Sunset

Her outstretched arms
Are the last rays to pierce the trees.
She gilds the West's windswept wings.
Over her bronze shoulder, her palette swings;
She paints the clouds. She mantles the seas.

She turns down the sun's amber sheet
And tucks in bird and flower.
She silhouettes hill and tower
And dances with sovereign feet.

She braids tangerine ribbon through
Heaven's cerulean hair
And blushes the surf's pristine cheek.
She puts the thrush to sleep
Then flees on her dusky mare.

Angel's Wing

Grace

Peace

Is

Having

The river's wisdom-

To carry the rain on your back with grace

Knowing the sea is your destiny.

Red Mittens

December air, the smoke of a fire

Memory on impatient wings

My father cutting wood

Face flushed like roses

The scent of oak

And the sound

Of the blade scattering splinters

Memory of my hands in red mittens

Grasping logs on the bottom stair

And the gentle voice

Telling me the air promised snow

And not to take more than I could lift

December air, the smoke of a fire

Memory on impatient wings

My father on a winter day

Snow on a Raven's Wing

A soul descends to the university of lies

And dons a robe of desire.

Ignorant of its former wings, crawls through fire,

Without wisdom and without eyes.

The ink runs dry in the writer's pen,

And the unfulfilled, white paper of a life

Lies waiting.

A widowed heart listens for familiar footsteps

That will never return.

Swift hours fall lame;

When will ecstasy again pain the senses?

All unfulfillments, errors, and transgressions,

Death satisfies, rectifies,

And apologizes for.

Hear Death's silent voice

Loudest in Joy's smug laughter...

Oh, hear Her sing.

With celibate hands, She mends all things.

Oh, hear Her sing...

Softly as snow on a raven's wing.

All that is born innocent

Dies soiled by living

Until Death cries and purifies

With cold fire.

Hear Death's silent voice

Loudest in Joy's smug laughter...

Oh, hear Her sing.

With celibate hands

She mends all things.

Oh, hear Her sing...

Softly as snow on a raven's wing.

All words left unsaid, all songs unheard,

All crystal summits reached for in vain

Are Death's courtesies, all of these.

Mists haunt November brooks,

Phantoms of summer past

Grieving the turning of time.

The drowsy bramble displays pearls of rain

On thorned, fruitless fingers.

The last generation of leaves

Is burled along the roadside,

A pauper's grave, crowded and wet.

Fire berries burn in scarlet hope

Until the first dispassionate snow

Fatally stings.

Can you hear Death's silent voice

In Joy's smug laughter?

Oh, hear Her sing;

Can you hear Her sing?

With celibate hands

She mends all things, all things.

Oh, hear Her sing

Softly…as snow on a raven's wing.

Heartwood

Lightning came, no one heard the fall

I am here tangled in the memory of roots

In thick underbrush, moss covering over

Earth reclaiming her own as it should be

Yet in the wet hours of night

I think of you, you of salt and earth

You who would take my heart and carve a new dream

You who would sand the splinters of fire

And buff my hard edges of mistrust

You who would take me and be gentle

With nail and rhythm of hammer

I think of you and your hands

Their sun-burned terra cotta and white stains of paint

Splattered like careless prayers

Sometimes heartwood must rot

And the carpenter's hands must remain empty

Each needing the other, a thousand seasons apart

Scarcely aware of what could be built in another time

Seraph

Summer morning

Sound of the piano drifting outside

Four years old, watching clouds

And listening to my mother's fingers dance over ivory

Voice shimmering like an angel's wing

Four years old, watching clouds

And reaching toward blue

Trying to touch heaven to my mother's voice

Gratitude

Hectic day, counting problems

Traffic jam, looking at the time

Hectic day, counting seconds

Traffic jam, funeral procession

Five minutes of cars with lights turned on

In honor of the dead

Seventeen year old girl laughing just two days ago

Mother burying her oldest

As May blossoms blow away into green

Mother not knowing what to do

With the prom dress

Or the dreams

Traffic jam, pause for silence

Beautiful day, counting blessings

Nostalgia

Only yesterday

Your hair caught the sun in its golden net

And your five-year-old smile was a blushing flower.

Only tonight,

After frolicking in your memory,

I realized you must be a woman now;

In a dream's passing, you were gone,

Golden child haloed by sunbeams.

Somewhere, far from time's insidious hand,

The children we all once were

Play in the wind-scented grass of a loved one's memory.

White Fragrance

Lineage

April holds out her cup of joy;

We drink her nectar of dark and light,

Sweet and deep fermented days

Dizzy with color and loud with desire.

We are in love, and so too, the world.

We languish in lush oasis,

Honeycomb bodies dripping with satiety.

Our lineage is infinite-

Lovers upon lovers flow in our veins.

This is our blooming hour of sustenance,

Our turn in eternity.

Microcosm

With the silken threads of the seasons,

Gaia weaves the tapestry of our days.

At the loom of Time, she braids the ages-

Each leaf, tree, stone...a thread.

Each heartbeat, breath, vision...a thread.

One thread severed from the whole,

Death of Nature, death of man.

Signature

Snow-dusted twilight, white constancy

Neighbor's cinnamon cat

Tip-toeing toward dinner

Pattern of paw prints

Across the porch

Chestnut Ribbon

I remember a woman

Drying her hair in the sun;

In a stream it dried in the wind

And shone like chestnut ribbon

Down her spine.

Fresh from sleep, I'd startle her thoughts,

And she'd give me a slice

Of her morning orange.

I remember a woman

Gliding in a cranberry gown

With lily-of-the-valley sweetening her steps.

I was nine

When I became aware of her beauty.

These sacred memories of my mother return

With the newness of impatient surf

Whenever I glimpse a crimson dress

Or smell oranges in the sun.

Legacy

Only a tree knows the life of a leaf-

The bud's crimson cradle

And the first brushstroke of green

On April's rain-dark canvas.

Only the tree knows the life of a leaf-

The summit of summer

Leading to long-awaited autumn;

Only in a leaf's gold death

Is its purpose fulfilled.

Its idle hours are cast into a breath of wind

And seasons of preparation unfurl into flight.

And the tree, having never had wings,

Births wings

And watches her children fly.

Oleander

My words are flowers in virgin light;

When you see me, you only see white fragrance.

You do not see the dark root,

The root so filled with want

It would poison your hand.

Crush the morning;

Rip me from the ground.

Spill my Julces until they burn the flesh

And I can finally touch the bone.

Snow Angels

The snow carves a cold blade

Into an onyx night;

We walk against the wind's diamond breath

Along the road lost hours ago.

I lean inside your corduroy

As we navigate the drifts in zigzag laughter.

"Do you remember our first winter?" you ask,

Folding me closer inside your coat

Until our footsteps tangle.

"Blueberry pancakes in bed, your velvet jacket," I whisper

memories.

We carve a road of laughter and wrestle in the white,

Your body burning over me.

Long pause, deep kiss, and over your shoulder,

Parting clouds

And a single star.

Vessel

There are nights inside of me

Stained with wounding

There are gardens of thorn

And mornings without hope

There are death camps

And ghosts of old hungers

I come to you hollowed, my soul carved by fire

I arrive, a phoenix after inferno

New and naked and trembling

I come carved by night

Empty to hold the dawn to your lips

Empty to hold the wine

That only comes

After the pain of the harvest

Homeland

Down a river

Of rapids and stone

Naked, unarmed, and tossed

Bound to flesh and bone

In search of an earthly title

Far from banks of rest

Enslaved to pride's bitter bridle

With wisdom the rocks scold and tame

Until the spirit directs its sail

Back to the sea from whence it came

Bright Darkness

Prayer

Give me a star,

And my life will bloom a heaven.

Give me a crumb,

And my spirit will find a feast.

Give me a drop,

And my heart will hold an ocean.

Give me a word,

And my tongue will sing the ages.

Give me now,

And my soul will be immortal.

November

Where's your hat, hearty little bird?

You color the winter-quiet like roses in the snow.

Not even wind-drift alters your bobbing flight.

The storm fills earth's November cup

Like blossoms falling in June,

Sparing your nest hidden in the spruce.

Gather your food, snowy little bird;

The voice of winter calls.

When you pass by my window,

I will remember roses.

Departure

I am going into the unknown,

Into the bright darkness within.

It has taken death to open the dream

Between worlds.

Do not look for me.

I am where the heart beats,

Where the blood flows;

I am inside you.

We are so close we are separated

By thousands of miles of consciousness.

Mentor

At this scarlet hour,

Quiet tree laden with blowing embers,

Teach me the song of crimson;

My rooted brother, sing your mantra of fire

And then stand before your lover, Winter.

Show me how to burn

And blind the air with light

Then live to tell my story in green.

Kindred

Cat purring to my heartbeat

Moment of perfect understanding

No explanation why I read poetry

And never read directions

Or wear moccasins in the winter

No explanation of her taste in mice

Or what she dreams of in the sun

Kindred spirits

Eden Unbarred

Willful curve of brow, chiseled grace of hand,

Bare strength of shoulder...

In my thoughts, you are a god tonight.

Each light and shadow of you is sacred ground;

Allow me this hour of idolatry.

I drink the river's thirst, and the river drinks of me.

River Lethe, Lover Lethe,

Naked and trembling upon your shore, I drink

And forget I've drunk before,

Forever wanting more

Of you.

Quench the body's flame, lest this soul turns to ash.

Plunge me into the rapids of honeyed oblivion,

Sweet god of forgetfulness,

Lord of the lover's wet fire,

God of my infinite desire.

River Lethe, Lover Lethe,

I have cried

I have died

To drink of you.

Tonight your memory washes my soul

A warm rain tasting,

Wasting

No part of my hunger.

I dissolve into the silent thunder of your waters,

Wishing,

Drifting

On the wet wave of your thirst

Until I am river as you are river,

Submerged as you are submerged,

Holy as you are holy

In this star-fired night.

My life

Opens to your whisper;

Petal by petal,

Dream by dream,

You bloom the summer in me.

Breathless, with beating heart, I look down

From love's snow-shawled summit;

I have never been this close

To life,

To death,

To love...

I forget all fires, all voices

Calling from the grave of futility

And let this bounty, this beauty,

This heat, this terror,

This summer

Rage in me.

Formless as breath,

Dreamless as death,

Cold and mute as stone,

I am but pain's remembrance

Without your forgetfulness.

River Lethe, Lover Lethe,

I have cried,

I have died

To drink of you,

Only to be reborn,

Baptized by your shimmering soul

That upholds my reflection like a lantern.

River Lethe, Lover Lethe,

Far from the blind earth above,

I answer your call;

You are Love…you are Love, after all.

And I have cried

I have died

To drink of you.

Lover and man I now hold within me,

Adam scarred,

My Adam found…

Eden unbarred,

And unbound!

Fragrant earth, unbridled sea,

And wind-washed heavens know

Inside this barren life,

This body weary and worn,

A woman,

A woman has been born.

Declaration

I am a woman

Who has birthed my own suns

Danced my own dreams

Conquered my own abyss

I am a woman who has tasted life

The salt of blood and loss

And the bitter honey of unanswered prayer

I am a woman who owns her soul...lock and key

Her body...breast and bone

Her mind...thought and vision

I am a woman who has tamed the shadow

Invented a new self...times uncounted

Woven a tapestry of memory

I am a woman only beginning

Having ended so many times

I am a woman who has been here

And there is a scar

Where my fire has been

Earth Psalm

O Great Sculptor of Seasons,

We bow to Thy altars of green.

O Haunting Composer,

We sing with Thy choirs of wind, wave, and field.

O Eternal Creator,

We thank Thee for Thy artist's soul.

Wood Smoke

Prairie Fire

Sleep abandoned

My life like a prairie on fire with you

Drought upon drought

Waiting for rain

Blazing from a spark

Thrown by your eyes

Dark skies

Flaming like dawn

Love untouchable

Sleep abandoned

Thoughts like a prairie on fire with you

Love untouchable as an ember

And hard as a stone

Sleep abandoned

Glowing

Knowing

I do not burn alone

Indian Summer

I will remember this day

Of windswept gold

And the monarch with blowing wings

Pausing to drink from a flower-

The lake, a sapphire brushstroke

And the family, a trinity of smiles on its banks.

They, too, will remember this day,

The laughter and the tiny fish thrown back.

I hold this hour of final fruition

Scented with coming sleep.

Day of beautiful dying,

Burdened with the anguish of the grape

Being crushed between the hours,

And in the blue perfume of her grief,

The promise of wine.

Ruins

You entered my temple with soiled shoes

Destroyed sanctuary, shattered the mirror

Vomited the offerings and killed the Gods

Get out

I will not be a beggar in my own palace

Autobiography in Driftwood

Driftwood, refugee of the storm

Lost child of the forest, soft heart

Made wise and beautiful

In the harsh womb of the waters

A survivor of remembrance, this wood

Burnished and all too human

A life like mine

Which lends its voice

To the Inaudible.

What we are, the wave has made.

Home

Our kitchen smells like my mother's-

Olive oil and garlic, rosemary and browned butter,

And the scent of basil,

Bright and impossible to forget

Like the sweet earth of her smile.

Muffins rise in the oven;

Dinner simmers in reds of bell peppers and tomato.

You come in from outside,

And your hair is pungent

With early spring and wood smoke.

I inhale all of you as your arms draw me home.

How long I have traveled

To this house by the river

And this kitchen

That smells like my mother's...

Unfinished Web

Hour of silhouette

As the spider spins in the dusk

The place where lost things go

And dreams abandoned at the loom

Unlike the spider who weaves to completion

We begin selves that never bloom

Oh, to be like the spinner so sure of her silk

So sure of her house of Self

With no thought of other webs

Lost to the storm

No thought of dusk

The place where lost things go

And dreams abandoned at the loom

Spindrift

Somewhere purple flowers bloom

In the sand with strong shoulders

To battle the whims of the wind.

Somewhere twilight leaves her deepest

Shade of blue and drapes a veil

Of mist over the ocean's cerulean eyes.

Someday I will be buried there

With my unbreakable, rebellious lover,

The sea...

Where time has overlooked and stars

Reach down with silver hands

To touch where the surf has ebbed...

Where I can die only to return

With strong shoulders,

A sister of the dune flowers.

Elysium

Upon an unknown path, during a night's wandering,

I happened upon the Elysian Fields.

Unaware of my presence,

The Gods drank sunlight and supped on dreams

Lost by mortal men.

Sappho sang by a perfumed pool,

And nearby, Orpheus made his lyre weep.

In an orchard heavy with nectar, Leonardo

Painted an angel with azure eyes,

And with hair blown wild, Ludwig accompanied

The blue thunder of a waterfall.

In the distance, cloaked in solitude,

Poe drifted into gold mists with his gray eyes

Drunk with inspiration.

Emily plucked lilies from a rainbow garden

And pinned them to her white-clad bosom

As Shelley and Bryon drank wine from wild honeysuckle

And danced with the Muses.

Whitman dreamed with a youth

In dew-glimmering grass,

And Woolf waded in the waves

As Isadora danced in the foam,

Intoxicated by the opium of the siren's song.

Long hidden, long I watched them,

Gods now ignorant of time

And earthly fame burning steadily

In the world behind them.

Upon leaving, I wondered who will be next

To dance among them;

Who could dance among them?

Metaphysics

Cloud becomes rain

Rain becomes river

River becomes ocean

Ocean becomes cloud

Seed becomes tree

Tree becomes fruit

Fruit returns to soil

Soil cradles seed

The end becomes the beginning

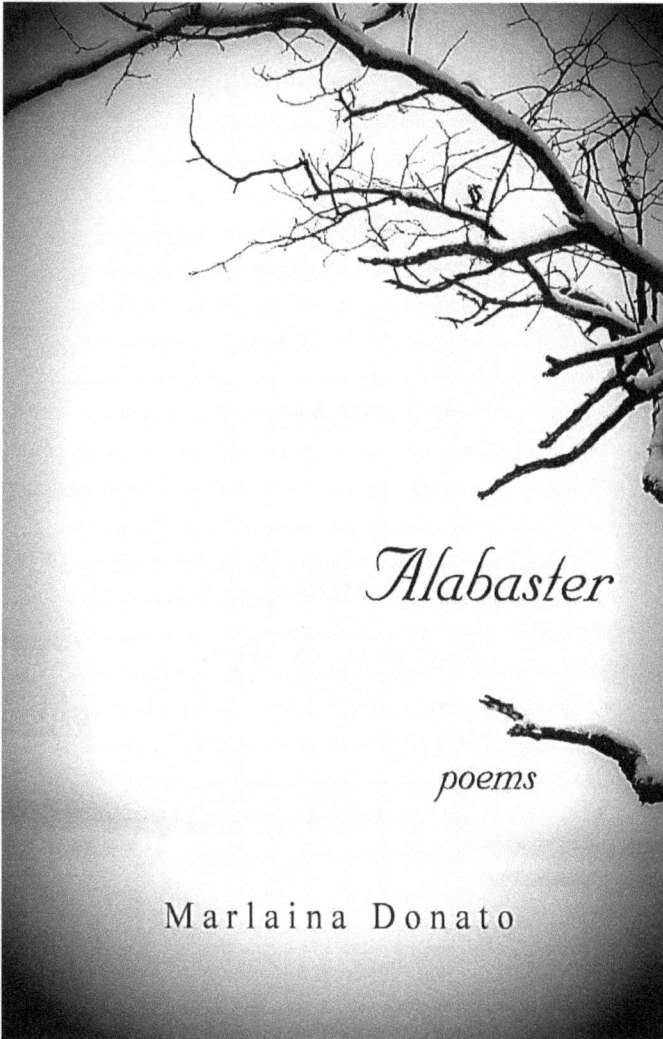

Alabaster

poems

Marlaina Donato

Alabaster

...for the winters of our lives

that teach us who we are...

Winterfires

Madonna

On this snow-hushed morning,

My four-year-old self is curled in sleep;

The room is smoke-tinged with burning oak.

She leans in to kiss me goodbye-

My mother in her amethyst coat with her alabaster face

Peering out from a halo of hooded fur.

Surely, she is an angel

Going out into a day deafened by white.

I fall back into dreams,

Knowing I will always remember her like this,

Madonna of the snows.

Compensation

A waning winter moon

Spills her heart into the dawn...

Pausing in death, she silently waits in the trees.

Consumed by darkness, she has dreamt

Of this heartbeat, this sunrise

She could not have seen in her youth.

Snowfire

The fire bleeds amber light;

Your hair smells like embers.

Lost in love's hour, we hadn't noticed the snow...

Now the steps are covered.

Lost in love's dreaming, we watch

The blowing white.

How am I to know

These moments, choreographed to your heartbeat,

Will be put away

Like leaves into a book of bitterness?

How am I to know

I will forget your hair in this light,

Its auburn scented with shadow?

That a forever from now,

On a morning haunted with ghosts,

I will open a book

And find the dead leaves of our season...

New Skates

Fresh snow patterned by new skates

A child and her father on the lake

When the years are collected

He will remember her green coat

With the silver buttons

And the plea, "Just one more minute?"

And she will remember him

Applauding an awkward turn

With pride in blue eyes bluer than heaven

Tundra

Soul under snowdrifts

Footprints of the old self blown over

No light casting a shadow of the self that remains

Idle in the indifferent fist of circumstance

It is forgotten that for every December

There is an April

Snow Angels

The snow carves a cold blade into an onyx night;

We walk against the wind's diamond breath

Along the road lost hours ago.

I lean inside his corduroy

As we navigate the drifts in zigzag laughter.

"Do you remember our first winter?" he asks,

Folding me closer inside his coat

Until our footsteps tangle.

"Silent Night sung in French, blueberry

Pancakes in bed, and your black velvet jacket,"

I whisper memories.

We carve a road of remembrance

And wrestle in the white-

Long pause, a kiss.

His body burns over me,

And over his shoulder, parting clouds

And the glance of a single star.

Circle

Alone, I take the old road.

The path is covered; leaves turn in their sleep.

December is an old woman,

And she passes me with gray eyes.

Where do they go, the hours we hold in vain?

Where do we go,

The selves that dissolve in dark water?

The heart is an old woman,

And she cries in the dusk.

The snows will cover us and the fires no one knew.

The forest will take us in

Without tears or regret.

New dreams will take root from the old;

Faith is an old woman, and she knows the way.

Millennium

New Year's Eve, after twelve

Last year of the century, a toast on the beach

And a pause of laughter

Wondering

Who will cast resolutions

Upon a sea drunk with moonlight

And shake stars from their lover's hair

A hundred years from tonight

We will not see another last year of the century

So drink my kiss, my lover with stars in your hair

While the year is so fragile, so new

And so too this desire

Inferno

A gold room, a pillow of thorns

Night deep in snow, soul on fire

This heart, a rose in a fist

Screaming to bloom

This hand pressed against the wall between us

Hour upon hour, year upon year,

Burning toward morning in vain

Praying for forgiveness and forgetfulness

Pause

I memorized your smile

As we walked in the gold after the snow

With a white dog pulling five steps ahead.

You were beautiful with your dark fire against

Winter canvas,

So beautiful you hurt my eyes.

I memorized your gloved hand

As we walked in the gold after the snow,

And the trees threw a puzzle of shadows

Against our silence.

A white dog turned the corner;

We paused.

A lifetime later, we remain there, at the corner,

My heart on pause

In the shadows

Thrown by the words you never said.

Winterscape

Moon pouring fire

Snow adorned with calligraphy of shadow

Night canvas

Violet brush stroke

Pastel morning

Wind and solitary cloud, a white smudge

By an unseen hand

In a Library

The only ones here on this gray, uninspired morning,

On the third floor,

We nestle in books and conversation;

We taste each other's words... living embers

Amid sleeping volumes

Whose sires dream beneath the centuries.

You tell me that someday my pages

Will be collected here,

And I assure you that someday your fire

Will shake the world out of bed.

We plan.

We devise.

We aspire.

On an ashen morning

Pale with orphaned ambition,

We blaze in the arrogance of our youth.

Gold Windows

Winter Sunset

The west is a mural of light,

The east, a blue wash of silk;

The moon is a rising opal

As children color the street with fuchsia chalk,

Concrete canvas.

Church bells ring as day's light drowns

In a twilight starred with gold windows.

Children laugh on this last warm day before frost.

Joy without a reason.

Slow Dance

Against your shoulder

In this shadow-scarred room

Against your chest

In this moon-pierced winter night

Against your belly

In this slow dance

Undress me with your thoughts

Run fingers of ideas along my spine

Do not touch me, just dream me

Dance me so close I no longer hear music

Only your exhale against my inhale

Let me forget myself

For minutes, hours, days

Against your sway

Midnight

We linger over midnight coffee

As we taste each other's words for the first time;

The city's heart breaks in February cold.

For a moment, I forget

The child who sleeps in a doorway

And the sidewalks stained with slaughtered dreams;

For a moment, I forget

Someone else's eyes that once found me

In the neon nights

And the sounds from the streets

That echoed up to our room, our bed

Overlooking the park.

For a moment, I forget

The last time I was here...

We linger over midnight coffee,

Tasting each other's words,

Being in this city, again for the first time.

Thaw

At dream's end, my fire will meet you,

Its heat no longer caged.

You will know

The hungers your eyes satiated,

The nights when I screamed your name into echo.

Only then, this deep river will rage from its ice

And all the words that dam my throat

Will mute even the song of God.

A Saturday in December

We walked through the holiday village

With coats buttoned up and shawls over our hair;

We looked like children, cheeks flushed with smiles.

Winding fences were strung with lights

And snow fell in whisper, fine as mist.

We shared dreams over a pancake brunch

At the inn on the corner

(Not wishing for the berries served when in season.)

We were content, that winter day,

With friendship's pageantry.

Bitter Honey

White door, stairs leading to an oval window

Stone hearth, old piano, bayberry candles

Entering through the old door

Expecting to find her, the girl I once was

Expecting her wide-eyed eagerness

And untouched soul

The willow chair, the yellow bedroom, the holly tree

All are here except the girl

Home for a spell, wars and lifetimes later

Home

So bitter, this honey

Scarred, this innocence

Soft, this wound of full circle

Through the Eyes of Winter

Behind a pane of silence,

A winter-eyed man watches the world.

He knows well the mischief of the squirrel,

Joy of an April bird feeder,

The quiet wisdom of the deer.

His silence is born from knowing...

The answers to his own riddles of fate

And the trifling importance of the hourglass.

In the lined, celibate skin lies a map of experience,

Avenues of laughter, detours of uncertainty.

Passion still quakes in the tired heart,

Now with a quieter voice.

In the grandfather eyes, the boy still skips

With an undaunted smile.

Tired feet have not forgotten how to run,

And the drowsy mind still dreams.

Trodding through snowdrifts of limitation,

The winter-eyed remembers spring.

January

A blue star hangs on the ear of twilight,

A heaven of heartbeats still to rise in an hour.

Westward moon, polished for her entrance,

Startles the darkness.

A silhouetted traveler pauses in step

And listens to the stars singing the night to birth.

Transience

The first snow drapes the earth's naked symmetry;

Somewhere, day is lit beyond the sky's pewter veil.

Birds leave prints in the uninterrupted white

Like those who alight upon our lives

Until the winds blow over them.

What do we have from these visitations

To prove their existence?

The snow preserves a print for only so long.

Beauty alights like a bird

And then she is gone.

Winter Amber

Red leaves entombed

In dark December ice

Autumn under glass

Rain

Through a long tunnel of days, finally, your voice

Our worlds touch

And I bear the weight of heaven

I love you, as the rain closes us in

I press your words against the storm

I love you, no need to choke on the unspoken

You already know

Yeats

You are a miracle, in your open white shirt

You and your hands more gentle than a verse of Yeats

You and your fingers pale and bronzed in this light

As the fire spends its wealth

We are a miracle, together on this winter night

A small universe sparking in the dark

My touch inside your open white shirt

More gentle than a verse of Yeats

Snowblind

November

November trees, skeletons of the year

I am here, a question unanswered

Past the point of sound, a syllable of silence

I have no language but a song unwritten

Street lights pierce the windshield

Left turn home to nowhere

Shout at the gods for someone to hold

Anyone

The man with the silver ring

The woman with summer eyes

Anything

A handful of dust

A pocket of light

Anywhere

The dirt road

The over-grown garden

The grave beneath 300 miles left behind

White

A slant of light on a white piano

Pale, beautiful fingers

Long and lyrical

Dancing over white keys

Pale, beautiful, loyal and living

Beneath the player's persuasion

No gold of sun, no petals of spring

White morning

White hands

White keys

A pause of white

New Year's Dawn

The winter dawn is a cup of gold;

Timidly, cautiously, the soul takes a sip.

A memory dances in the light...

Broken wings remember the flight;

A memory dances in the light.

Morning shimmers with gold, soon to die into silver;

For a dream, the earth is young,

So young, a shadow could break its heart.

The Bridge

I see her standing on the bridge

During a morning snow.

She does not offer a word;

Our eyes brush,

Joy's poverty in her glance.

I smile...

This morning is broken-winged,

But there will be a day of rejoicing,

Dear sparrow in the snow,

A day of rejoicing.

Preservation

I watch you read in front of the window

Halo of hair, pale-painted mouth

Blue tumble of sleeve

All silver-lined in virgin winter light

Quick flight of thought and wire-rimmed glasses

Answering the sun in reflection

Artist's hands and the gentle turning of the page

The lifting of rain-blue eyes for a pause of smile

You are more than a man—half fire, half shadow

For a breath, you are the morning's canvas

Forever preserved in the memory

Of a woman who loved you

Window

In cold pre-dawn fire

A star burns in the East

A candle in some distant window

Inaudible

Veined leaf, once green summer on your cheek

Now blood-stained russet

The sun burns toward winter

Leaf-heart, slowly starving for light

Knowing the certain end, the anemic fall into the wind

Screaming in colors translated as joy

While the inaudible rages beneath your gold

And the sun burns—heedless, deaf, and fat on eternity

Avalanche

Old woman, time-ravaged skin

Clinging to the bone

Hair a white wisp

She waits in the hallway

In a graveyard for the living

As they change the soiled sheets

And talk in Spanish

Old woman with eyes like mine

Who once drank wine under the stars

And laughed when she got caught in the rain

And loved someone she can no longer remember

An old woman pleading to go home

As I pass her on my way out

Old woman with eyes like mine

Alabaster

Winter night chiseled from alabaster

The day unraveled, your body undressed

Hunger unfurled on white linen

Elegy

Autumn doe beside the road

Curled in graceful death

Once beating heart now mute

Beneath wind-weighted grasses

Forests will remember you

And the hills that wore your tracks in December

Coat turned silver for the snows

Cast off like a tired dream

While your soul nestles somewhere in summer

Somewhere far from this highway grave

Sleep

Beautiful dancer

Sleep

Spent

I came to you late in the season

When you were burdened with years

And your flowers and fruit had seen their hour-

I came to know only thorns,

Unaware that beneath your snows

A beautiful summer had once been there.

Winter-Speak

Encased in ice, I have learned to speak winter.

Sentenced to snow, I have surrendered to cold chastity.

But in the heart of this tundra,

Behind stone that cannot burn,

A fire rages in your colors.

Resigned to paralysis, I have married stillness,

But in the isolation of nights,

Behind stone that cannot move,

I dance barefoot to your summer.

Buried in white sleep, I accept the sterile harvest,

But in the wasteland of want,

Behind stone that cannot hunger,

I ravage your orchards.

Enshrouded in futility, I inherit compromise,

But in this prison of silence

Behind stone that cannot speak,

I sing

I sing this love.

North Wind

Manna

Pages yellowed by time

Stark words etched in ember

A signature—a pirouette in ink, right hand corner

Her name untouched, her spirit long flown

No longer the name of my mother

But the name of a woman who spun words

Blood-stained words of light

A woman

A glorious sun burning in verse

A forgotten poet singing to her daughter

Who holds her words like bread

In a time of famine

Bread of dark sustenance

Of grain that says, "I too hungered."

Bread for these dark nights

And dawns with no answers

Ending

Dry fields are bleached by winter's breath,

Dry fields raped by time

And corn bending in death.

I stand at the rim of the world

As night comes in on fire,

Broken shards of ember over harvest waste.

I stand at the rim of the world

And watch you die in the sun.

The universe seeps through

The hole gutted in the center;

The ground is a river where you bleed out of me.

Dawn will rise; spring will dance;

These fields will again know lover's green.

I stand at the rim of the world

Knowing your heart has no return.

The sky turns toward ash and sleep,

And I own nothing, nothing

But the wind blowing through where you used to be.

Price

The sun retreats, igniting long-dead leaves

In amber resurrection before the first fist of snow.

The sun retreats, spilling eons of solitude traveled.

Who or what do you look to when you too need light?

Who waits with lantern in hand

For those who make their own light?

Exit

Winter's final snow bonnets the world...

Crimson buds shiver in dreaming

And the white-gowned hydrangea is a lady in lace.

With the season's closing, you leave my life

As you entered it, during the last snow

Before spring's first whisper.

I will continue onward and with each milestone,

Pause to remember our laughter;

With each year's closing snow,

I will see the hydrangea wear her lace

As my heart, cold and proud,

Wears the beauty of your memory.

Snowrose

My footprints make a pathway to your grave;

Sounds of the city trespass the heavy iron gates.

How thin the thread

Between worlds, realized only now

As my boots violate the chaste night snow.

The first snow remains on granite

But has vanished from the soil

Covering your memory.

I leave you a crimson flower

As a nearby angel watches

And dons winter's first white on her wings.

Venus

Venus is a burnt opal

In the corner of sky above the church;

On a night like this, long ago,

Our laughter punctured the darkness

While the world slept

And Lady Guadalupe smiled.

Far, how far it is since

That cold street charred with piñon,

That mural of starlight,

And the plans and dreams spilling from plenty.

It is familiar, this penance of bliss,

Its thorn through my soul

And the sound of church bells;

It is familiar, this prayer,

Pressed like a burnt opal to my chest

And its unanswered futility.

Ritual

A lone bird drifts in the wind,

Painting silhouetted freedom

Against a pewter sky.

Others gather, and in the pale smoky light,

One, two, three...still more,

Circling above fallen, bloodless leaves,

Soaring in ritual,

Death dance.

Memory Keeper

Snow-crust and the dialogue of our boots

Along cobblestone

Bells from the old church and your breath

Against my hair

I will not forget these things

Or the color of your scarf like crushed sapphire

I will not forget my hand in your back pocket

As you tell me the history of this city

And where to find the best croissants

Will you remember this when we are old...

Remember holding me against the wind

And how fragile, how indestructible

You have made me?

I will not forget these things

Or the color of crushed sapphire

As you hold me against the wind

Sea Glass

Winter sea of broken glass

Crushed beneath the weight of gray

Inside, wrapped in the summer of your arms

You feed me with marmalade fingers

Laughter over a late breakfast

Tea amber in the cup

Blue eyes faceted with light

Contentment

Threshold

Heaven's heart weeping white

Trees in royal slumber

We stand in the threshold

Longing to fly into the night

To walk until dawn

Newness too beautiful to scar with boot prints

Pristine pause of time

It is enough, this threshold

And heaven's heart weeping white

Morning Walk

Your body is a moving prayer

In this brightness, holy hour

Of light and lover's arms breaking the winds

Arms strong as the distant mountains

Imposing in violet

Beyond the crushed petals of water's edge

Kiss, an epiphany of warm oblivion

In this brightness, holy hour

Love making all things new

70 Degrees

Winter quit his job today

And spring dusted off her dancing shoes

The sun came back a hero

And left his autograph across the hills

The winds reveled in the heavens

And birds gossiped about winter's breach of contract

Leaves played tag across the lawn

And every tired heart remembered

What it is like to be in love

Winter

Embraced by the North's infertile breath,

Winter arrives with yew braided in her hair.

Barren, she is akin to Death,

'Tis poison fruit her sable tresses bear.

Look for her eyes in the blue of a December twilight

And quietly listen for her trailing gowns.

When the moon wears a halo of whispered white

'Tis then she empties her purse of frosted down.

She bejewels the trees when the year is new

And buffs the lake for sharpened silver blades.

Morning sun ignites her prism's hue,

'Tis why we forgive her heart of spades.

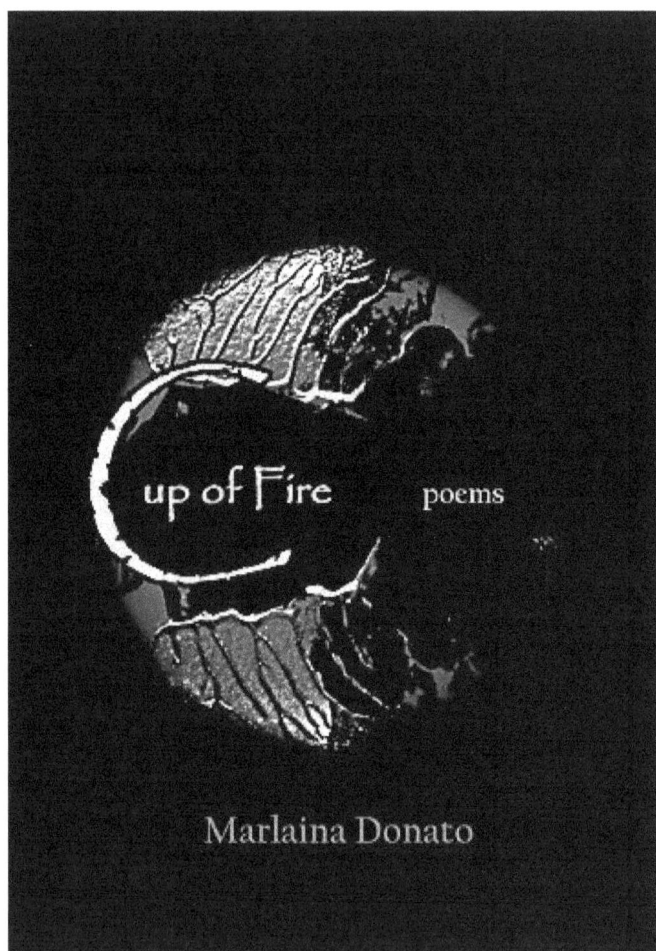

Cup of Fire   poems

Marlaina Donato

Cup

of

Fire

Thunder's Edge

Pomegranate

Desire like an open pomegranate
Rapture like cold morning water
Drawn up from the well of night
Beauty dappled and winged
Out of the cocoon of want
Desire abundant and for the taking
Desire not without price or struggle
As the explosion unearths the gold
As the blade yields the nectar
So too this ecstasy

Not Yet Found

Where October drifts by
In a crimson veil,
I listen for a footstep
Inaudible beneath a century of Autumns.
Lover, who would have been
Yet forever will be,
I look across the barren plain of time,
Hungry to hear your whisper
In the falling leaves,
The dying dream of another year's end.
I turn from October's fevered cheek
To discover your eyes
In the gray ghost-rains of the night,
The smoke of far-away fires,
The moon's silver breath
Upon the brow of the waters.
Longing for eyes once lost
Yet never found,
Love that could have been
Yet always has been,
Lover whose gray eyes overstep centuries to wash my soul
Of its dark seasons.
Gray-eyed rain, wash my dreams tonight,
Dreams that can never be
Yet, forever, will be…

Salt

Our bodies wear the waves,
Desire buoyant upon the tides;
We thunder
Hunger
Toward home.
You taste like the tides
And my tenth summer
When the sea left its salt in my soul;
Tenth summer, dark waves whitened
On midnight,
I wondered what was within
The sea's wild and wailing heart.
It was you,
Dark and wild and waiting...
It was this ecstasy, this letting go
Of the bottom,
Becoming you, dissolution.

Blue Smoke Morning

Blue smoke morning
Moonstone river, opal city
Hiding us
From who we are out there
In here, only the essentials:
Books and a bed
And a hunger to match the two
And on the wall, a mural of our
On again-off again
In here, room for all the selves
Too numerous for out there
Come back to bed, my Hindu god
With eight arms to hold me
Eight arms to hold the eight of me
Without explanation
Eight arms and incense soul
To love me to silence
Love me home again

Daybreak

Sixteen seasons of cold and darkness
Waiting for a flicker of dawn
From your eyes
Sixteen seasons of famine and drought
Waiting for this morning
This heat, this sun
Heart finally drinking the light
Recognition
Morning crowded with travelers
Only us, only us
And a thousand birds
Singing in your eyes

Amaryllis

You drink the night from my body;
Which is deeper,
Your thirst or my thawing?
Only ecstasy knows the depth
Of this well,
Ecstasy pulled back like scarlet petals
In the urgency of blooming.
Only a flower understands this opening...
I am a hundred doors opening,
A woman birthing, unearthing fire,
Amaryllis unfurling.
Only love knows
The famine of this fulfillment.
I am a hundred rivers thirsting
A woman birthing, unearthing fire,
Amaryllis unfurling.
You drink the night from my body;
Only dawn knows
The sacrifice of this surrender.
I am a hundred mornings rising,
A woman birthing, unearthing fire,
Amaryllis unfurling.

Matches

Heart famished
Feast and sustenance granted
Yet hunger rages
What more could possibly be given
Heart playing with matches
Burning the hours
Spoiled, greedy child
Deaf to discipline
Yet so fragile
Shivering in your corner of need

Destiny

I look into eyes and remember
A forgotten mile,
A heart's unexpected turn
On the way to this morning...
One goodbye less, one step further
And I would have missed forever.

Poison

I would die for you,
Die so you can live in this heart,
This heart that shuts you
In its tower of secrets.
I feed you shadow
And quench you with shame
Until you are fat with emptiness.
I would die for you,
Die so you can live in this fire,
This fire that burns your myrrh
To the gods,
Any god what would
Grant me your touch.
I would die for you,
Not knowing I already have,
A million selves
In the grave of your hands,
And you are now eternal,
Immortal
On the poison of this ambrosia.

Visitation

I feel the cloak of your arms
Comfort me through the years,
The hours that drag their feet
Like stubborn children,
Moments that fly into a lost forever.
Take me with you into the storm
And let me taste thunder unafraid.
I open the secrets of my soul,
This fragile box of flesh
In which they are encased.
I am young, but the anchor of time
Weighs upon the wings of youth;
Yet tonight, I own the skies
And soar against your wilderness.
This night will remain
A shimmering pearl of memory
Among the ashes of a life.

In the long,
Idle eternities of our desperation,
Love visited us.

Oasis

You began a drop of rain,
A whisper of wet;
You are now a storm,
Thunder in my blood.
I began a desert,
A shadow of thirst;
I am now an oasis,
A garden
Should you hunger.

The Dancer

You writhe in the dance,
A small universe against the floor.
I watch you and wrestle with your beauty, muscle and
bone,
Hungry to be the ground beneath you,
To be cold and indifferent,
Unreachable and silent
Beneath your small hands,
Hands that could split
My soul in two…
Hungry to be blind and numb
To your open thighs
And the Eden between.
Beautiful universe,
I watch you and tremble inside
The muscle and the bone,
On the edge of flood.
Now I know
A gesture could create a world
And beauty so untouchable,
A river of whispered prayer.
Beautiful dancer,
I kneel at your Shiva-soul
And bathe in the Ganges of my tears.

March

We take the path along the river,
Chopping through half-melted snow
And dark chocolate mud.
Our boots crunch and slosh
Over the iron bridge
With the Pollack graffiti,
Past the wetland and sleeping frogs,
Toward the waterfall's silver thunder.
Our shadows pause
Every few hundred feet
Against the day's shattered gold.
The sky is so blue it hurts my eyes,
And the earth pulses
Beneath our boot soles.
Shield me even from this beauty,
In the circle of your arms,
Against your neck;
Hold me at the thunder's edge.
Beloved, hold me
At the rim of the world
As I hold the song of the river
That is your heart
Now beating for me, for me
On this day
Of shattered gold and cascading silver.

Ember Nights

Arrival

Twilight shakes blue petals
From her hair,
And the moon scatters
Her broken pearls over the river.
The hours dress in their finery
As I reach into the twilight
And pluck a star
To wear as a trinket;
My soul puts on the party gown
Never worn,
And all of night celebrates your coming.

Now That You Are Gone

You are so much nearer to me now,
Now that you are gone;
How easily I can grasp your hand
From the stars
When once, I had to reach eons,
Even when I was in your embrace.
I love you more now,
Now that I no longer love you;
My thoughts return to you
With such quality, such feeling
Now that those thoughts occur
Occasionally rather than continually.
As autumn comes back,
I remember you
Even more vividly than those times
Actually spent with you.
I see you everywhere
Now that you are no longer here
Obstructing my vision.
How much more passion
I have for you
Now that my heart is cold.
I love you more now,
Now that I no longer love you.

Spice Market

Drumming in the streets
Amber woman drenched with dancing
White hem trailing in the dust
Moroccan nights wavering like stars
Kneeling to dine
Men with obsidian eyes
Wearing age or desire
Serpentine paths stenciled
With footprints, signatures
Of countless lives
Heady air haunted
And dizzy with spice
And women's voices
In the procession of passion
I walk alone
Knowing how our bodies would fit
Beneath a moon
More beautiful than youth

Raven

Stranger with eyes like the night,
Eyes of someone I once loved,
Angel with the raven's eyes,
Sit next to me.
Laugh like sudden rain;
Laugh like someone I once loved.
Our nights will never meet,
Yet for this hour
Flood the drought while I memorize
The dark invitation of your hair
And the bronze hands
That would feel like desert wind
Across this barrenness.

Gold Hunger

The fire's gold hunger
Has paled to ember;
I hear the footsteps of the dawn.
You lift your head
From my heart
As we seek one last breath of fire
Before I leave.
Intrusion of daylight
Remains unpardoned
In this eclipse of desire.
Morning waits
For this bitter honey
To fill the thirst
And dark eyes to pale to ember;
Then I scatter into the dawn,
Heart a startled bird
Into the pain of light.

Moon Upon Wave

The sea shimmers in the moon's
Half-empty light.
With each wave's turning
The light flames silver
Then goes out by foam.
With each star's burning
Night dreams on the billows.
At this hour of Love's yearning
My soul
Walks
With your soul.
Lost long,
Long lost,
I reach
Love's earning.
As moon presses upon wave,
I am pressed to you,
Breathless, deathless
In Love's learning.

Burn

In the wake of burning,
You turn to me in the moonlight,
Your hair a flame in the darkness.
You smile a smile only I know,
Only my body knows...
So pure it lives but a second,
A drop of snow put out by my touch.

Winter night, playing my six string,
Fingers against steel strings
Giving voice to hollow heart of wood.
Hands tire with song, remembering
Making love to you until the burn.

First Night

This night, a leaf in amber
Your beauty imprisoned in memory
Voices of the stars between our bodies
My lips bruised from your hunger
First night
Wrapped in your fire
First light
Morning trembling with memories
Your name, first word
Unspoken, unheard
Absence of pain
Beautiful stain
Of bliss
Having loved you
These hands now holy
Peeling an apple as if the first
First thing tasted since your kiss
Tasting, not wasting
A breath of this
Sweetness

The Flower's Rage

Sleep, savior to the wound,
Tempers the slow hunger of nights,
But what blunts the edge of day,
The slow hunger of the day?

The light cuts with truth:
I am not your lover.
I am not your blood.
I am not your friend,
Not even your enemy.
But a flower crushed
Beneath your step,
A flower
That once longed for
Recognition
From sightless eyes,
Dreamed of being spared
Against your breast.
Could you ever know
The flower's worth
Or the flower's rage...

The moon knows,
Bleeding fire
When the soul
Is an empty cup
Never to be filled again
With the light

That hesitates
On your brow
Before igniting dark eyes.

The gnarled pine knows,
Stenciled in scars
Against the dusk,
Young moon
Climbing its branches;
This twisted dancer knows,
Imprisoned in futile grace.

This heart knows,
This hard, rocky earth
Upturned, ripped, softened,
And opened to receive the seed.
Days of long sun
And rains of grief
Until succulence and swollen sweetness;
A million lifetimes beating
Within its labor
Only to come to
The end of the season
To find the harvest
Will not be gathered.
There is no hunger to receive,
No waiting mouth,
No parted lips
Leaning toward fulfillment,
No emptiness striving

For completion.

You are dead
Yet among the living,
Pulsing with beauty and elusion,
A wave dissolved at first touch,
A star too far, too cold
For human hands.
Damn you, take me...
Take me
Out of nights of want.
Take me
Into your dark fever.
Take me
Out of solitary flight.
Take me
Into captive infinity.
Take me
Out of destiny.
Take me
Into chance.
Take me out of the war.
Take me
Into the dance.

Burn me
With the ash of the dream
That was you.
Feed me,
Feed me the fruit of your lies.

Sleep, savior to the wound,
Tempers the slow hunger of nights;
But what blunts the edge of day,
The slow hunger of the day?

Night Rain

The rain's cool breath
Disturbs the curtain.
Is it a lover coming to call,
Have you found me,
Lover who burdens me with desire
At this fragile hour?
I have yet to press my longing
To your breast
And drink oblivion from your kiss;
O, pour your soul
Into this hollow hour
With the remembrance of your voice
More beautiful
Than a choir of angels drifting
Through the rain.
Hold my quivering life,
Its light and shadow,
The silk and the thorns,
And I will be for you
What the sheath is to the sabre,
And I will be the curtain
That moves to your breath
For an eon of nights.

Dark Moon, Deep Kiss

At an Art Opening

Laughter overflows
In a room crowded with words;
In a blur of conversation,
I am torn between listening
And locating your presence
By the door.

Then your sudden smile, a flower
Opening to my sunlight
...Hello...

Morning

Day emerges
From a cocoon of snow;
Dawn spills over
As we eat your pancakes
By the window.
Your hair is still wild
From the storm of my hands,
And you smell like maple syrup
And love.

Night-Bloom

So this is what it would be like
If Fate had given us a full harvest,
Both of us at evening's turning
Each bringing
The day's experience
For the other to examine;
Exchanging thoughts
After the book is closed,
A slow kiss over burgundy,
A smile antiqued
By a candle's gold,
A brush of hand between words.
But our hearts fell upon thorns;
Our love will not reap orchards,
But a single flower
Born in impossibility,
Each petal a miracle
Awakened in darkness.
This flower
However small,
However fragile,
Is perennial.

Pilgrimage

He moves inside me
Hard rhythm of storm
I move inside him
Soft ocean flame
Undertow and morning sun
In this bed of Eden
We journey to God
A pilgrimage of flesh and prayer
Dance of grace

Dionysos

Along a pathway of moon
We run with new wine in our veins;
We dance, sandaled in visions,
God of the Dark Thirst,
God of the Dark Nirvana,
Find me with eyes
Of amethyst fire
And hair that waves black
As the river.
Fill me with ecstasy
That has never known the sun.
Pain me with joy
That has known suffering.
Entrance me with music
Wilder than your leopards
Crouching in the shadows
With intoxicated eyes.
Anoint me
With your soul's first pressing;
Feed me your kiss of bittersweetness,
Kiss of wine and myrrh...
All days of bright bliss
Are sacrificed for one night
With you,
God of the Dark Thirst,
God of the Dark Nirvana,
Lord of the intrepid seeker
Who seeks you tonight.

Yin/Yang

Your black boots
With a million miles
Branded
Into the soles
My red poet's blouse
With a maze of laces
Your hungry fingers
Have no time for
Your voice, sweet smoke and brandy
Copious with words
Mine,
An E-string on a guitar
Slightly out of tune
Your body,
Light as water
Flowing over
The heavy curve
Of my driftwood
Clothes, voices, bodies
Weaving
Such harmony of opposites

Dark Moon, Deep Kiss

Dark moon, deep kiss
Diving into oceans
Beneath your tongue
Your hair spilling gold
Into my touch
The darkness trembling
Bodies braid then burn
My soul, a naked flame
As you shatter my depths
With bare hands

Cardamom

Reason to ruin, senses drugged
A kiss, a fragrance like fire
Nights like cardamom
Serpentine trance
Blinding seas
Nights like cardamom
This is what they died for
Killed for
Discovered new continents for
Hungered for
One breath of spice
Against the tongue
Wine would never suffice again
After monotony, madness
At any cost
Nights like cardamom
My name burning on your tongue
Whisper more precious than gold
Nights like cardamom

Flowers in the Storm

Night wind
Through the half-open door
Rain and waves, a thousand drums
Scent of flowers in the storm
My body, thawing spring
Rain-soaked with your desire
Ecstasy torrential

Black Denim

Silhouetted against city light
We kiss goodbye
Against a darkened door.
We still have yet to touch
For the first time,
But not yet, not tonight...
Let me sleep alone, content
With only the thought
Of your denim
Against my bare skin.

Ruby Glass

Slow dance to Spanish music
3 a.m. and the air smells like wine
A breath of sea
Through an open window
Candles shivering in ruby glass
Intoxicated by your words
Against my throat
Desire too deep to disturb
Dancing to flamenco guitar
As the wind blows
Our bodies shivering
Like candles in ruby glass

Ember

Mist like ash
Morning sky silver before sun
Maples half burning in October gold
Arms circled in silence
We walk after love
Bodies still pulsing
So alive
We can hear a single leaf
Drift to wet ground
An ember extinguished

Downpour

Wash my soul
In the dark rain of your hair
Rain on this night
Resounding with your silence
Drink these secrets
Beneath my kiss
(Let me have this dream)
Drench me with words
You will never say
(Let me have this dream)
My only wealth
In this night of poverty

Rain Pool

We whisper, afraid a single word
Will startle a heaven of stars
Caught in the dark mirror
Of a rain pool.
You cup your hands
For me to drink,
Your heartbeat tremors in my veins
And in the cool, wet abandon
Of your fingers upon my thirst.
My life, withered
And threadbare by the ages,
Opens and drinks starlight.

Drinking the Storm

Last Day

I imagine myself sitting,
Wearing a purple dress
With an open book
Across my knees
And a maple tree lit with sun
Beyond the porch swing.
O, to die in May
With poetry in my lap
And your smile in my memory.

Envy

First taste of wanting
The flower's opium
First taste of needing
The flower's poison
First taste of hating
The flower's sunlight

First Spring

Our laughter drifts
On a rose-colored wind
As we waltz down an avenue
White-washed with blossoms.
I want to leave this life
Dancing in your arms
When all the world
Is lit with your smile.
The day tries to hold spring
Against its dappled breast
As the aged clutch at memories.
An old woman limps across
Our rejoicing...
No band rests on the spotted left hand;
Widowed hopes sleep
Beneath her withered surface
Of seasons.
She is a gnarled reminder
Of a tree once towering
In the twilight.
Spring returns with blossomed enthusiasm while she sits
Without a single branch to bloom.
She finds no more purpose in flowers
And keeps her gaze to the North
Where all barren things
And ornate springs
Cease.

Vignettes of April

A child's laughter
Rises above the fountain
Like water spray
As a young woman sits
On the church steps, wind blowing
Her auburn against the sky.
We take our bikes
Through the city,
Wheels scattering
Pink rain of blossoms.
We study stained glass
And speak of angels
With my hand in your back pocket.
Avenues of open flowers
Shouting crimson
As I chase your desire
To the third floor
Memorizing Sunday sun
And April in your eyes.

Short Story

She sits three benches away
With pewter hair and a tweed coat
Carelessly buttoned.
Morning sun breaks through
As we invent her life…
How beautiful she once was
As she carried her sketch book
To meet him between classes;
He would read her
His latest chapter
Over coffee and croissants,
And she'd brush his hair back
To memorize its sunlight.
Through marriage
And three daughters
Only a single painting remained
In an attic of memories
And abandoned quests.

A young man sits across from her
And she suddenly remembers
His face.
Could it be…
For a flicker, she dreams.
No, he would be old now, too.
We stand to go,
Contemplating the end…
She asks him the time

Just to see his eyes,
The same blue without the fire;
No eyes ever burned like his.
We laugh down the street,
Glancing backward.
Instead, the young man perches
On his bike;
She does not glance up.

Will people weave stories
About us someday
When we are old
And could we ever live up to them?

Beginning

Morning, an hour old
Eager and spending light
New arms radiant
This love just born
Every breath the first
Every goodbye the last
Every word a touch
Too beautiful to voice
Genesis

Saffron

I wake to the sound
Of church bells
In the valley
And the scent
Of last night's wine.
The back of his neck,
Just where the waves
Touch the bone,
I inhale the scent
Of earth and bread and honey.
Sunday morning,
With my body
Pressed to his,
I wake to the sound
Of new memories,
Last night's words,
His whisper
Like a feather falling against
The darkness.
We make love to the sunrise
Then walk into a saffron day,
Drunk on gold.

Refuge

In you, new harvest
In me, a soul hollow with rot
In you, heaven's blowing silk
In me, the knee-deep mud of Hell
In you, a table of bread
In me, hunger of a thousand nights

Forgive me for entering
Without knocking
Pardon my heart's unkempt mess
Overlook the torn years
And dirty dreams
Disregard eyes that look too long
And blood-stained hands that cling
Give me a bed and sleep's dark kiss
Give me shelter until morning
Until these bitter winds
Die over the mountains

Triangle

I did not know
One night of fire
Would turn into
A wish for a lifetime
And the years Fate granted
To someone else...
The nights of music,
Children's rooms
Lit with laughter,
And the rose-patterned dishes...

Cappuccino

City dawn, a gray flower unfolding
Orchestra of cars
Day's curtain opening
Spotlight of sun
Morning jazz and your smile
Kiss, languid, endless
Cappuccino getting cold

Tempest

The waves are wild tonight;
Driftwood is testimony.
With broken wings,
Through miles of tempest,
Youth flies back to me
Searching for shelter.
But there is no harbor here
In this heart ravaged by wisdom.
You walk beside me
Holding scattered petals of the years;
Let me look away,
Let me defy their fragrance;
Let me only remember thorns.

Night Jewels

We sat near the street
And you blew into
Your cinnamon tea;
We shared
A chocolate strawberry
Knowing it was a kiss goodbye.
We talked while the wind
Took our laughter
And passing cars blew your words
Against me.
In that light, you gave me your eyes;
You slipped them to me
Like stolen jewels.
We sat near the street
And I denied the coming morning
And its four hundred miles.
In that light, I gave you my heart;
I slipped it to you
In the envelope of my life
If you should ever want it.

Unlocked

Solstice moon, holy and heavy
Over our aching
Hearts like desert flowers
Drinking the storm
During the long drought of my youth
Had I only known
The coming of these rains
Desire ages into love
The last door in my heart
Unlocks and opens
Welcome, my beloved
May you stay a lifetime

Eros

Thou hast pierced me
With thy arrow of light,
O, great prince of love,
And left in my heart
A wound of gold
And took from my eyes
My mortal sight.
Prince of love, where am I to go?
For I have eyes no more;
Thy way is dark, thy wound is deep,
But I am grateful forevermore.
I am blind and hurt,
But both are sweet.

Silk and Thorns

Flicker

He brushes past me,
A quiet comet of light,
His hair is dark earth
And in his sweat, the salt of its soul.
I weave the hours of the day,
Scrubbing the harvest
By a window,
Glancing up to glimpse
His passing,
Noticing the hands
That have known heartwood
And the love of a good woman.
Hours of simmering scents,
Weathered wooden spoon
And warm bread,
A flicker of longing,
Sampling the thought
Of him,
Eating the dream
Of impossible nights.

Concerto

Our words flutter against the moment,
Hurried streams of laughter.
You in crimson
With your gypsy eyes
And the concerto of light
Playing on your bottom lip
As you speak.
You tell me the finches
Have made a nest in the fern
And the difficulty
Of watering the soil
Without drowning the eggs
Not yet hatched.
But all I can hear
Is the concerto,
Memorized note for note,
Year after year,
With the constancy of finches
Who come back.

The hours burn white and quick;
I see them etched in your skin,
In my hair's silver beginning.
When I was a child I dreamed
Of growing old with you,
Of your heart's ember in mine.
Eons since the dream...
After beating Fate with futile hands,

Surrender.
Our words flutter against the moment
As our tea gets cold
And the finches fuss above our heads.
Blessed, these hours that burn
White and quick
And your face more beautiful
Than memory.
Blessed, this fate
And growing old together;
This way, the only way,
Like learning to water the fern
Without drowning the eggs...
Careful and slow the stream,
Like love long unspoken,
This love, the only love
That can stay.

Invocation

Day of thorns
Soul, barefoot and tired
Shut the door
Invoke sleep with your name
Alone at last
With the thought of you

Reflection

Your child
Will never sleep in my womb,
Child who would be given
Your eyes
And their sweet smile of sadness.
I will never watch him
Become your reflection
Or when I am old tell him
How I loved your hands
Or about the night
You played the piano
By a candle's half-whispered light
While the world was lost in snow

Diamond

With one glimpse of your eyes
My life's dying blooms into living;
The spring bud slain by snow
Bursts into resurrection.
With one glimpse of your eyes
My heart's abyss ascends into light;
The scattered ashes burn
Into phoenix flight.
With one glimpse of your eyes
My life's prison opens into sky;
The stone soul shatters into diamond.
With one glimpse of your eyes
My life's dying blooms into living.

Judas

I have eaten at your table
And filled my emptiness.
My hand has touched yours
In the same bowl.
I have drunk the wine
Of your presence
And hungered for the bread
Of your body.
I would sell salvation
For the silver
Of your passing touch,
And I would deny you
Three times before the dawn.

Flood

Dream me awake
As we lie in your bed.
Your skin is a language
My soul knew before this life,
And the morning rains gold
On this fragile remembering;
Your arms, at last, the harbor.
I empty the years-
The desolate and futile,
The broken and raging years,
Into your vastness.
Infinite sea, I flood into you,
This river of long-aching.
Drink of me,
Take me to your depths
Until I struggle for breath
And the morning pours gold
Over your arms
That have become my eternity.

Impasse

We walk to the rhythm of waves,
Words just out of the reach of pride.
We travelled the depths,
Too sure of breath.
The sun continues to beckon,
Offering beauty of the horizon,
Unaware your heart
Has gone to sleep.

Ghost

On a night that lifts your eyes
To the stars
I will return...
I will be the wind
That blows across your body.
I will be the earth
That cradles your step.
I will be the dream you half remember
When you kiss the dawn
From her mouth.

Fool's Gold

You walked in carrying a memory,
The memory of your eyes
Plucking my gaze like a bird
Into a net;
The memory of your hair
Blowing gold in summer light,
And how I gave the entirety
Of my being
For your small smile across the world.
You walked in carrying
These remnants of us.
Now divided, we speak from
The safe shores of distance.
Morning sun leaves
A breath of bronze in your hair,
And my heart remembers
The value of fool's gold.
Silence resonates
Between the empty canyons
Of our words,
And winds blow through the hollow
Of our abandoned nights.
And I remember;
I remember.

Night Cry

Laughter across the way
Pierces the rain as I wait for sleep,
But tonight, sleep is a stranger.
Three thousand miles of circumstance
Lie between us.
Tonight I know you are not alone,
And sleep is not with you, too.

I sift through possibility
Searching for a sacrifice
That could buy us tomorrow,
But the Fates place no value
On pauper's dreams.
Tonight I know you are not alone,
And sleep is not with you, too.
Someone else holds
The password into tomorrow
With you,
The one who cradles
Your whisper tonight.

Deep River

At dream's end,
My fire will meet you,
Its heat no longer caged.
You will know
The hungers your eyes satiated,
The nights when I screamed
Your name into echo.
Only then, this deep river
Will rage from its ice,
And all the words that dam my throat
Will mute even the song of God.

The First

With my heart's wine outpoured
For careless thirst
And my body's bread
Broken for hollow hunger,
I accept your bed this night.
Against your soul,
I press the soul never given
And the second innocence
That waits at the end of experience.
Lover who is not the first,
Beloved who is last,
Lift my soul's elusive veil,
Beloved, who is first...

Breath of Jasmine

Divinity

Within each soul
An angel sleeps,
Nestled in oblivion
Until a lover wakes its dreaming.
Tonight your angel
Looked through your eyes
And my angel embraced
Through my arms.

What is love
But the awakening
Of the divinity within ourselves?

First Summer

The day is like warm clay in hand,
Hours molded by nimble fingers
Of conversation,
Matter-of-fact like your ready humor
And my eruptions of laughter.
Our first summer in terra cotta,
Patterned with small joys
Fired in the kiln of this love.
At day's end, fireflies burn like meteors
And we reach for the day's pottery-
Cups of new memory, clear and cool,
Sweet as long-awaited rain
That heals the drought.

Jasmine

A white wall
Wears a necklace of shadows,
Blue thoughts scattered by the sun.
Morning heat pulses like fire;
I watch a carousel of passersby,
Ecru and scarlet.
Your words are the only breeze
Wafting like jasmine
Over my listening.
Summer burns her last hour
As we sit in the shade
And an old man travels the dust
Murmuring to angels.

Constellations

We sit in your car
With the top down
And collect constellations
In a jar of memories.
Too busy with words,
You miss the gold star
Falling
From heaven's highest shelf.
Your laughter
Catches
In my hair
Like this desert wind,
Blowing
A remnant of youth
Into the jar...
Then another dart of gold
Dancing
Across the sky
As we sit in your car
With the top down,
The night crying stars.

Watercolor

Outside, the wind
Disturbs a kiss of snow.
We embrace by the fire,
Your hands warm with apology.
Day blends with night.
Twilight bleeds into autumn white.
We, too, merge...
Breath rising,
Brown hair blows into black.
We merge...
Hearts drumming.
Scarlet of passion and blue of soul.
Violet unity.

Ode to Sunset

Sunrise,
The virgin of the morn...
Sunset,
The bearer of nightfall...
With love,
A bridge of noon is born.
Beloved sunset, your colors of splendor
Will soon fade and grow old.
Today my rays are youthful
And today my rays are new,
But someday, I will be there with you.

Beloved sunset, your colors of splendor
Will soon fade and grow old,
But how I long to kiss your lips,
Your lips of dusky gold.
Please wait and leave behind
A trail of scarlet light,
And together, we will enter
The starlit night.

Within the Reeds

Wind and reed entwine;
Man and woman embrace.
Idle lake, the sky's looking-glass
Mirrors the wind-scattered heaven...
Upon a stage of summer blue,
Cloud dance.

Initiation

Beneath the night's starry wing
I offer myself.
I am perfumed with your soul,
Soul of amber, breath of jasmine.
Tonight, I will be initiated
Into your Mysteries,
Lover deified by desire.
I enter mortal and will leave immortal.
I will leave adorned
With henna and gold,
Invisible until a wind
Blows my garments
And startles the morning with jasmine.

Beloved

Lover, press my petals to your desire
So I may weep my fragrance
And anoint your divinity.
I drench you with rains
Long withheld...
You drink
As parched earth drinks spring.
I have wandered through
Night's labyrinth
To taste this light-shimmering hour
Shining through the prism
Of your smile.
In the eye of the storm,
I dance until my soul
Splinters against your thunder.
Haloed by sun, we shatter
And dissolve
Until we become less than breath.
Beloved, press my fruit to your hunger
So I may bleed my ecstasy
And offer my divinity,
For this hour,
If only this hour, I am immortal.

Circle

You have pressed your life
To mine before;
Your eyes are not new,
Eyes that startle me
In the night with remembrance.
Your soul is still a trembling wick
At the end of a star, and your smile is still the sun's
Wandering brother.
I would still ransom tomorrow
For your kiss in the rain
Or to be a wind-tossed leaf
That blows across your path
On your journey back to me.

Eden-Heart

I have tended this garden,
This Eden-heart for four decades,
Ripped poison roots
From beds of dreams
And pruned back to nothing
To make way for the wine.
I have shred my words on thorns
For a single taste of fruit
And nursed meadows of inspiration
Until they burst into song.
I have tended a single bloom
From infancy,
Extraordinary, one of a kind,
Haunted by its fragrance in the night,
Certain I will not outlive it.
And now, this flower, here at my feet,
One of which I have no knowledge...
This cup of fire
Scorches the bone,
And I long to touch
Its forbidden center.
Adam passing through,
Brilliant and gleaming,
Untouchable,
And it is enough.

Wind's Turning

I thought I saw you,
Barely touched by the years.
Three steps behind you
In the deafening crowd
I thought I saw you.
Would you have known me
Beneath this painted mask of time?
Would your heart have remembered,
If only for a second,
Like a jewel of sun on water
That glimmers and glints
And then is gone
With the wind's turning?

Eos

Just beneath the surface of sleep,
Your smile tastes like sunlight
And your soul is full with morning.
Come to me, angel of the hours,
Into the temple of my heart
That holds the altar of your beauty,
The book of your eyes.
Beneath the surface of waking,
Before this life,
I gave you the key to my nights
And my shattering.
Open me, angel of the dawn,
Open me.

Incense

Beneath your fire, I am incense
Gathered, prepared,
Bitter resin
That burns in sweetness only once.
O, release me
From this dark box of time,
Reserved not for a saint or a deity
But for your burning eyes,
Holy, honored guest of my soul...
Beloved alchemist,
Turn the bitterness of this life
Into fragrance and burn me well.
Burn me well.

Bitter Fruit

Stillborn

Like the others,
I carried this dream
Year after year
Through decades of fear
Not enough earth
Too many graves to dig
No space for yet another
O, let it be, let it rest
No purpose
For milk in the breast
Let it be, let it rest
No purpose
For love in the breast

Blood Muse

From a shadow across your cheek
I sheltered a thousand dreams.
From the dust of your dance
I built a civilization of ideals.
From the sun in your eyes
I painted the grace of God.
From your indifference
I composed a rage
That taught the thunder.
From the sword
Of your touch never given
I gutted my own soul.
From your heart's shallow cup
I burned in famine.
Dark heart, there are no more hopes,
No more nights,
No more lessons to learn
Except how to close the book.

Black Ribbon

I do not remember
The exact day we died,
But I remember
You were wearing
A light blue shirt
And the wings in your eyes
That once carried me home
Were broken.
I searched the man
In the light blue shirt
For the lost fire,
But all I found
Was morning sun
Resting on two cold hearts.
Today,
We live separate realities,
But somewhere,
We still walk together
Unburdened by impossible dreams.
Somewhere we live
Out the future
We risked everything for
That never happened.

The last time it rained
I saw us run by
Beneath an umbrella;
We danced to our song

That played on the radio
Last night on my way home.

We haunt beaches
And rose gardens,
Unaware of the black ribbon
Pressed to our photograph
At the bottom
Of a remembrance box.

Ten Years

After a decade, a glimpse of you
Your face turned,
My heart still not safe
From memories blooming
In forgotten soil.
A glimpse, your back turned,
And I remember never holding you;
A glimpse
And I am young again,
So young I believe
My single touch
Could dissolve your stone.

Requiem

Defeated, the sun goes down,
Wounded and bleeding scarlet
On the cold battlefield of the west.
I mourn its passing,
But who mourns for you,
You who have left my life?
No one else attends this mass,
Only memories
Cloaked and candled in the dusk
Around the dust
Of who you once were.

Ember of my first fire,
Tear of my first sorrow,
I search your ashes for a well
To quench the virgin desire
Still sparking in the night.
Singer of silence, I listen
For your second-coming,
But you left my life as you entered it,
A soundless star scarring the earth with frigid heat.

Beautiful ghost,
You hold the heart of my youth
And the wound you made.
I still tremble for the love you,
The pain of you,
The chasm of lives

Never to be mended.
The years have left scars;
And my soul is bitter fruit.
What a strange harmony,
Love and hate,
And how the child who loved you
Still struggles to remember
The words to an unfinished song.

Goodnight, goodbye my friend.
I leave you lilies
If you should ever glance backward.

Winter Garden

After a thousand dreams,
I am here again in your light.
After a thousand dreams,
Pain dies against your smile,
The deep pulse of dawn
I cannot taste;
I cannot touch;
I cannot own.
(The garden wears winter,
Unaware of this season of fire.)
After a thousand dreams,
I am here again in your darkness.
After a thousand dreams,
The pain is reborn with your smile,
The deep pulse of night
I cannot taste;
I cannot touch;
I cannot own.

Anniversary

Soft and full of miles,
You fit me with the ease
Of worn leather.
How long it has been
Since the dawn of us...
My love, you are the one
Who taught me thunder.
How good it is to feel
Your eyes reach into mine
With their old knowing,
Knowing the journey
Even before I tell it.
Sit with me
As light washes in
And finds the blue of your eye
And the line of your cheek
Rough with morning.
Sit with me
As you always do
And fold me
Against your chest;
Let us sit
As we always have
Until we are
A tangled knot
Of thoughts
And words
And breath,

Longing to find
The core of this fire.

After all is said and done,
After the end of the end,
It will be us.

Sit with me;
Rock me
Against your words,
Your voice more beautiful
Than I remember
All those years ago,
More beautiful
Than anything
Worth remembering.

Cage

My heart, wrapped in your absence
Waits...
For a breath, a smile.
In me, love's impatient wings
Thrash against the cage
Of this unending dream of miles,
And I envy even the wind
Against your cheek.

September

We walked after the rain
Into a sapphire night.
We talked about small things
We would forget by morning
And pointed to stars
Burning through clouds
That would live only an hour.
But when I am old
I will still remember
The ballet slippers I wore
Into the street and your sudden smile
When the wind blew my shawl
Against your hair.

Second Chance

It has been years
Since we blushed the moon
And shamed the stars,
Ten years
Since I remembered
How you bounce your heels
When you are impatient
And how poppy seeds
Get stuck In your teeth
And how profanity
Sounds like Shakespeare
On your tongue.
Ten years
Since I remembered
How I look at you as if
You've just created the world
And you remind me
That you didn't
And how our bodies
Split the atom
And it is still never enough;
Ten years
Since I forgot
Where I was driving
Because I was dreaming about
How you smell like honey
And how your tenderness
Jewels my senses

And how much I love
Getting mad at you
When you remind me
That you were right
All those years ago
About how much I love you,
And someday, someday,
I would remember.

Deliverance

Hunted by the wolf
And shunned by the stranger,
I clung to this foreign soil
And my bitterness grew.
On nights when tears ushered sleep,
My soul asked for you.

Rewarded silence
And sheltered by indifference,
I sought a gentler place
When storm winds blew.
On cold, quiet mornings
Waiting for sun,
My heart asked for you.

In search of words
And vineyards of truth,
I listened for those who knew.
Groping in forests of wisdom unfound,
My mind asked for you.

Shackled in solitude
And tired with thirst,
I pressed the fruit
Of fulfillment in vain.
When ecstasy withdrew
From my futile grasp,
My body asked for you.

Mosaic

Between blind chrysalis
And triumphant wing,
Between the stupor
Of disillusionment
And the sobriety of answered prayer,
I waited for your footsteps.
You came during the darkest night
Of the soul,
Your smile a small dawn.
Mosaic of morning inlaid with light,
I welcome you,
Trembling with awakening.

Fire Flight

My heart
On the precipice of you
Sunrise burning the edge
The taste of a thousand dawns
Beneath your tongue
The rhythm of a thousand nights
In your eyes
My heart
On the precipice of you
Out of the cage, without a net
Sudden flight into fire

Legacy

Beneath this ocean of starlight
We are a pulse
In the night's beating heart,
Milky Way spilling stars
Through the ages
Blessing centuries of raptures.
The night is ancient and will pardon
Our youth and this idleness.
Tonight, there are no books to write,
Miles to exhaust,
Or hungers to satiate;
Only love must be attended to.
The night is ancient
And we touch on sands
That hold the bones of our elders,
Lovers, all of them,
And it is love they remember;
It is the only thing.

Last Touch

5:30 a.m.

Dawn comes in whispering light
Ten minutes before the alarm
I stir into his arms
In the half light,
Eyes closed
I know him by heart,
Know the scent
Of moss and honey
Just where his hair curls
At the base of his neck.
I know him by heart,
The citadel of chest
And soft cheek;
I know us by heart,
The soft intersection
Of thigh and knee,
The effortless tangle of half-sleep
And "I love you,"
The song of morning's half-light.

Eden

This terrain, rugged and smooth
Earth and wind, water and ember
This new continent
Formed by lava and sea
Moving as if with glacier magnitude
His body

Compact and certain
In his grace and his heartbeat
This terrain is familiar and wild
Soft meadows of sleep
Thunder and darkness
All that he is beneath my reverence

Last Touch

Another spring night descends
With wings of rain and remembrance.
Somewhere, you listen,
Waiting for my return.
For a moment, I hear your heartbeat
On the wind;
Sweetness drifts in through
The half-open door,
And you send one last touch to me.

Twilight

Peaceful twilight
Neither day nor night,
Thy heaven's still,
Neither dark nor light.

Silver moon,
Crescent in the west,
Cast thy beams upon my breast;
Lighten the corridors of my heart
With his infinite song.
Take the sunlight from his shoulder
And create my spirit's dawn.

Sleeping Endymion

Shadows of the winds
Dance across your sleeping eyes,
The light, a chisel
Sculpting your being.
But who holds
The instrument that creates you?
Who is so great, so beautiful
To bring you forth?
Surely, you are God's masterpiece.

I love you, I whisper.
Tonight, unafraid, facing the wind,
I love you.

Phoenix

Here the heart's journey ends
Here
Infinite search
Becomes Fruition
Here
The journey ends
In this bed of fire
We rise again
Phoenix lovers blazing
With the sky on our backs

Pardon

Snow falls in whispered constancy,
Pardoning the world
And its soiled heart,
Falling in whispered prayer
As you gaze out a window
In your half-buttoned white.

Beautiful friend,
Your soul steals my breath,
Your soul, soft as the light
Across your breast,
Soft as snow falling in white whisper
Beyond the window.

I have known your eyes
For seventeen winters
Yet today they are new,
New as the year and the world
In this pardon of white.

Beautiful man,
I have traveled the world
And its soiled heart
To find you in this heaven light,
The rain of silver prayer
As you gaze out a window
In your half-buttoned white.

You are so new, fragile glass
In this awakening,
This soft shattering.
Snow falls
And so, too, this heart,
Blooming, breaking,
If you will have me,
If only for this hour of pardon.

Soul Memory

I have never known
Your arms
Yet they have held
Me for lifetimes.
I have never
Witnessed morning
In your eyes,
Yet I have studied your face
In a hundred dawns.
You are so new
Your voice is not yet
Distilled into memory,
Yet I hear your words
In my own heart's beating.
You have not been here
Long enough
For me to grieve
Your absence,
Yet before sleep,
I whisper
Your name in tears.

First Winter

Flicker of winter candle
Midnight and steady snow
Our bed with the chocolate sheets
And the cradle of your arms
Hour upon hour
Your dreaming warmth
Against all of me
Half-sleep, turning toward
Your whisper, "I love you so..."
Blue morning and the taste of coffee
Beneath your tongue
And your open shirt
Like the sustenance of warm bread

Storm's End

We linger across ancient cobblestone
Our footfalls lost in the centuries.
We cry against morning's gray heart.
Bound in stone, an angel looks on,
Dispassionate without
The sun's illusion.
The sky breaks its vessel of rain;
We run beneath a doorway,
Warm mouth against warm mouth,
Shoulders dappled with tears.
Cobblestone glistens like agate,
Morning leans toward noon,
Sunburst.
Terra cotta landscape
Dreams in apricot.
In a deserted courtyard,
I am in your arms,
Music drifting
From a second story window.

Vow

Today, I give you my heart,
Relinquishing all fear of tomorrow.
Today, I give you my trust,
Discarding all doubt.
Today, I give you my dreams
So they may nourish
Your hungry hours.
Today, I give you my faith
So I may know God with you.
Today, I give you my love
So I may be a better person
By loving you.
Today, I give you my body
So it may be an instrument
Of my love.
Today, I give you all the selves
I have been,
The self I am now,
And the selves I will be.
I give you my hand
So we may dance through life
In laughter and in tears,
In bounty and in deprivation,
In continuity and in change,
All the days of my life.

The End

We walk a gray autumn beach
Wearing old conversations
Long outgrown.
Tireless, the arms of the sea
Reach
'Round clusters
Of mossy stone.
I lean my head
In your hands...
We can't go forward.
We can't go back.
We can't stand still.
As the sea
Whitens the sand
We cover old topics,
Laugh and pretend,
And then fall silent;
No use to go on,
We've reached the end.

Canticle:
A Modern Song of Solomon

He is beloved, Friend, Lover;
There are worlds
Beneath his tongue,
Liquid sun,
Ember nights.

He is humble as the soil;
Like roots invisible
At first glance,
Deep and tangled with wisdom.
He is quiet sustenance,
Wild and spinning prayer.
There is song
In the shadows of his face
And a canticle
Of dawn
In his eyes.

In the close-curtained reverie
Of my thoughts,
I recite the litany
Of his being.
He is only a man;
I am only a woman
Clothed in the miracle
Of his smile.

My desire burns
On the ocean
Of this love,
A flame without wick,
Without end;
It is an invisible sun
That will live
When my flesh is no longer his
And his flesh is no longer mine.

I dip my breasts into morning
And his mouth
Fills with daybreak.
His breath is pomegranate;
His body, honey and storm,
And I am drenched
With satiety.

He is husband, my soul-divided.
He is the wealth
Of all my days,
And each hour spent
In his dappled light
Endows my eternity.

Trinity

The sleeping heart is empty,
The awakened is glad,
The wounded is wise.

But we must know each-
The sleeping, the awakened,
And the wounded-
Before we can say
We have truly loved.

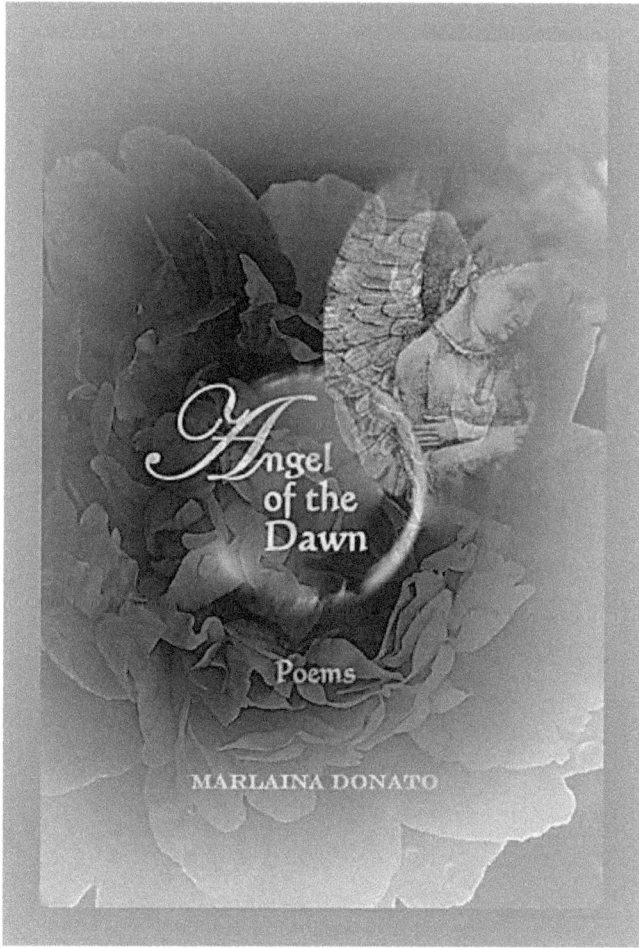

Angel
of the
Dawn

Poems

MARLAINA DONATO

Angel of the Dawn

...For the angel with the shining sickle
who severs the flower, and in its grave, sows the seed of
another more brilliant than any before it...

Translating Ecstasy

Synapse

Go
Where God's lute
Wafts through the corridors of a deaf world.

Go
Where discontent
Empties into oceans dissolving regret.

Go
Where Beauty is born
From a single thought
Stretched across imperfections.

Birth

Life is a series of deaths...
Every hour, something stops breathing-
A dream
A fire
A belief;
A heart stops beating.

The final death-
Feared
Prolonged
Mourned;
The final closing of the book,
Rarely seen as the birth
That ends all deaths.

Angel of the Dawn

Just beneath the surface of sleep,
Your smile tastes like sunlight,
And Your soul is full of morning.
Come to me, Angel of the Hours,
Into the temple of my heart
That holds the altar of Your beauty,
The book of Your eyes.

Beneath the surface of waking,
Before this life,
I gave You the key to my nights.
Open me, Angel of the Dawn;
Open me.

Heart's Turning

Wind washes the morning clean,
Baptizing a soul battered by dreams
And faces sleep never forgets.

In the cascading wind,
One remaining leaf
Leaves the branch.

A dream lets go.

Promise

The soil is prepared...

Winter-numb earth
Upturns into a fertile womb
By the pain of the plough.

Does the field,
Stripped
And
Burned,
Know of the bounty to come?

Orpheus

Bow to string
Hand to instrument
Once a tree in a wind-swept forest
Now reincarnated into symphony

Flesh upon wood
Hypnotic alchemy
Each giving the other a soul
Translating ecstasy

Hour of Flight

Follow the path of shadow
Where memories lean into the water;
Do not be afraid to touch the river
And its dark lips whispering night.

The truth is- we die many times
Before we are born again.

Take the morning's smile
Strewn across the heavens...
Play with it; take its freedom.
The dying is over.
Trust the bright coins of dawn
And buy an hour of flight.

A Million Selves

A flower has been ripped from the root,
A flower that will not bloom again;
But you do not know
An eternal garden lives in me...
A garden so vast, so infinite,
Heaven is but a shadow in its hand.

A self has been shattered,
A self I will never again be;
But you do not know
A million selves live in me-
In my Soul that is greater than birth,
Wiser than death,
Stronger than *this,*
Your fist
Your greed.
I will not bleed
Your memory.

Joy

Joy lives in the river of tears;
A nymph enclosed in the water's depth,
She tends the fires of forgotten smiles.
Her throat is pearled with memories,
And her voice sweetens
The river's bitter miles.

Holding the warmth of the coldest rapid
And a lantern for the darkest wave,
She leaps over rock and pitfall,
Harnessing the rainbow,
Adorning the soul's empty cave.

When tears flood the banks,
Clear are her prism eyes.
From the mud of despair,
Her torchlight gleams,
And thrown a coin of faith,
She will rise.

Creature Kin

I am the serpent.
See the world through my eyes
And wear a hood of wisdom
When you walk through the underground
Of human nature.

I am the eagle.
Borrow my wings
And drink the sunlight
When you aim for uncharted skies
Of potential.

I am the cheetah.
Run with me
And brush the shoulders of the wind
To temper your power
With moral grace.

I am the snow leopard.
Seek my summit bed
When your mind is drained
Of answers
And the inner sage will awaken.

I am the owl.
Know your nocturnal path
And forgive and see beyond
Your illusionary darkness.

I am the butterfly.
Remember my modesty
And the ability to drink the moment.
I am the chameleon.
Remember my secret
Of survival
And my instinct to wear experience
Like a shield.

I am the ant.
Remember my determination
And willingness to work
With others with focus and humility.

I am the loon.
Remember my song in the night
And the medicine of solitude.

I am the lame gull.
Remember my persecution.

Dark Sustenance

Autonomy

Tiny spider sleeping
Magnificent web netting a sunbeam
Tiny spider sleeping
In a home she built from a thread

Who thought
You could accomplish such magnitude
Such symmetry
From your own being

And so too the soul
If only we remember

Ostara

Leaf, blade and blossom
Bear the scars of snow.
Earth giving birth
To green.
Mother Eternal,
You offer your breasts of rain.
Tree, flower, and grain
Bear the memory of snow.
Earth giving birth
To herself,
Mother Eternal.

Vesta

Chosen by birth and initiated by fire,
She has tended the altar;
Year upon year, night upon night,
She has introduced incense to flame
And offered the first fruits of her soul.
A lifetime of rehearsal so easily dissolved
In the poverty of preparation
When the god, at last, arrives...
Can a life ever be ready for the glance
From immortal eyes?
Can a heart not quake
Beneath its own desire?
Can a cup not shatter
From its own fullness?

Journey Back to Innocence

My feet reach terrain never crossed
And rocks unforeseen
In search of innocence lost.
Heaven and Hell, a heart drifts
In between.

I am a stranger here
With no map in hand
Or shoes to conquer the stone;
Yet I know this foreign land-
The soul, the flesh, and the bone.

Long, I have been a child out In the night
With a canteen of dreams
The darkness spilled.
But here, the stars are bright
And my wings cannot be stilled!

My steps are bloody,
Yet they defy the thorn,
And wisdom warns to turn away.
Heaven or Hell, a heart is torn.
Which must I obey?

Thirst weakens will,
And the wind persuades thought.
A clear pool beckons in the mist.
Against this cage, my fear has fought.

I duel with tear and fist.

I weep and wade in the water's quiet eyes.
Though, I have bathed in the mighty sea,
Here, I am baptized,
And my lost reflection embraces me.

I am That I am

We are living flame,
Hearts born of fire,
Souls sired by the stars.
The only ones of our kind-
And the last.

Irretrievable

Day's jewel shatters in the west.
Night plummets between
The sharp edges of birdsong.
April continues to bloom-
Inspiration or habit, only she knows.
While the spirit, a broken lute,
Remembers a song
It will never sing again.

Legacy

Pages yellowed by time,
Words etched in ember.
Stark in their light,
Glowing but leaning toward death;
Her signature- a pirouette of ink,
Right-hand corner.
Her spirit long-flown,
Her name unremembered,
No longer the name of my mother
But a woman who spun words
From blood-stained silk.
A woman, a glorious sun
Burning in verse,
A forgotten poet singing
To her daughter
Who holds her words like bread
In a time of long famine.
Bread of dark sustenance, of grain
That says, "I, too, hungered."
Bread for these dark nights
And dawns with no answers.

Second Birth

How fragile, how frightening
This hour...
Silent flower
Lifting her face after the storm.
Life hollowed by pain
Now empty to contain
Only this beauty.
How fragile, how frightening
This absence of rage...
A flower opening her eyes after frost;
After devastation, nothing lost.
Youth, love and grace regained.
With wisdom, all attained.
First birth- learn to walk, to cry.
Second birth- learn, earn to fly.

One of Ten-Thousand Names

Goddess spoke to me
In the voice of the wind,
And I learned a different song.

Goddess gazed at me
Through the eyes of the moon,
And I became beautiful.

Goddess touched me
With hands of twilight rain,
And I was healed.

Goddess found me
On the battlefield of broken dreams
And held me in Her arms of peace.

Sanctuary

Muse, you have been here;
Here in the fragile dawns,
In the morning deer,
In alabaster snows,
In the birch against the blue...
I will remember you
In this room,
In the sun's gold goodbye
Through cold glass,
In the ecstatic lapse
Of time
Between scars,
In the oak leaf's falling
And in the answers
Of the stars.

Night Waters

Ascension

Blinding darkness
Our souls spilling backward
Catching a wave of fire
Extinguishing into
Pulse
Heartbeat
Sun
Lovers into Beloved
Awake! Cocoon of flesh forgotten
Hearts, the weight of a dream
On the breath of Now

Chrysalis Outgrown

Lightning scars the ashen cheek of sky;
Silver light bleeds into the blowing cloths
Of the wind.
Barefoot on parched grass,
I cast off my soiled scarf of dreams.
I undress my life
And stand naked before the storm.
Hair once bound now tangled
By the thunder's furious hands.
Heaven's pewter cup brims,
Quenching thirst of grass and skin.
I laugh at the umbrella once clung-to
As my breasts drink the rain,
And into the storm's vehement embrace,
Cast all of myself.

Requiem for a Star

In the night's voiceless cathedral,
Legions of stars burn steadily,
A distant dais of prayer candles.
Somewhere, the birth of a new star,
A newly-lit wick,
Is celebrated while another dies,
Beaming its light without encore
Or ovation,
Bequeathing eons of prayers,
Generations of wishes
To the unheeding darkness.

In a crowded night,
Who notices the candle gone out?

Disciple

God of my soul, prophet of my pain,
You arrived like the dawn,
Bearded and bronzed in the gleam
Of the corridor's end.
With eyes that harbor heaven,
You hold my life like a dove
In Your sun-clenched hand.
Into love's tentative sea,
I cast faith's gold-woven nets
Of constancy
And gather wisdom,
Harvesting until the nets break.
And my heart, walking on water,
Shimmers and dances like diamonds.

Soul-Quest

Famished, searching for sustenance,
The soul seeks another soul,
But its image remains unfound,
A heart beating among strangers.

The Fish

He glides through night waters,
Outwitting a maze of shadows and lilies.
While the others grapple over morsels,
He wonders what the moonlight is-
Silver rain, ring-less and mute?
Lilies of light floating like stars
On a watery tapestry?
Surely, the moonbeams
Are the boat lights of angels...
No, they are celestial arrows
That wound with longing for answers
Or wings.

In an Old Church

Morning scatters a galaxy of snow
Over black-limbed maples
In soldier's stance.
We walk through the meadow
Once haunted with June butterflies
And breeze into the old church
On the corner.
Wind presses its cold cheek
Against the windows,
Eavesdropping on a century of prayers.
Nearly a year's soil beneath our footfalls,
Seeming a lifetime amid
The blowing stars of snow,
Amid the white-winged ghosts
Of butterflies.

Familiar

Cat purring to my heartbeat
Moment of perfect understanding
Words superfluous
No explanation why I read poetry
And never read directions
Or why I wear moccasins in winter
No explanation of her taste in mice
Or what she dreams of in the sun
Kindred spirits

Madrigal

Sapphire hour
Closing doors of the day
Silent walking
Pause
Listen
A madrigal in the twilight
Wind chimes blowing
From a house somewhere
In the blue

Citadel

Stripped even of myself,
You are all I own-
Womb of my birth,
Beauty of this earth.
In your arms I have survived.
In your arms I will die.

There is an army coming to plunder,
Coming to rape.
I am without sword, without escape,
But I have my fist
And the key, the Me
They will never find.
Sanctum never to splinter or fall;
Stake, break, take all-
Never to surrender, only remember
This Faith, this Fire, this Infinity...
Sanctuary, sanctuary;
Between yesterday's blown-out flame
And tomorrow's unseen face,
Beloved or burning sky,
You are safety's last embrace.

Beloved or burning sky,
My pain is polished
In the gold fury of your fire,
And my soul will forever rise
From your desire,

Phoenix eternal.
You are all I ever owned...
Womb of my birth,
Beauty of this earth.

Prism Garden

Magnolias After the Rain

I exalt Life-
The gross matter which encumbers me.
So, Death do I pardon
For hesitating to answer my request.
The rain is sweet on the bough,
And I am here to witness
Spring's timeless glory.

At the Crossroads

I came to the crossroads of Self
Where an old woman spun white threads
And moonbeams ran down their lengths
Like spring spiders.
I offered the Fate who determined
The length of life
Sweet wine of praise,
But she continued to spin,
Moonlight spilling off her wheel like
Water.
I danced for her and gathered fruit
Of faith and sentiment
In exchange for a thread
That could wrap around the earth twice.
Tired and bewildered by her silence,
I stepped closer
And saw that she had my eyes.
Her hair blew in the midnight wind
And shimmered like moonshine
On the willow that dwells
By the river.
I stepped closer
And saw that the smiling, weathered face
Was mine.

Magdalene

Out of the tomb,
Out of three day's eclipse of the soul,
You rise, enshrouded
In the shining garments of the morn.
From the Void, you fly back to me.
...Rabboni, Rabboni...
I reach to touch the life
I may no longer touch.
You have risen only to entomb me
With longing.
...Rabboni, Rabboni...
After you ascend, my hands
May then touch your feet,
But when you return to me,
Your spirit will be aqua glass
Blown by the heavens.
Near your beauty and fragility
That will no longer bear
The weight of my love,
I will bow to your divinity
But mourn the man
Whose sandal remains
Imprinted in the dust
Of one woman's heart.

Daughter of the Phoenix

Fire will forge my death
And fire will forge my birth.
I stand beneath the sun,
My destiny foreknown.
In ash I will die;
From ash I will ascend.
As my mother and her mother,
I am a child of the phoenix,
Daughter of the flame's auriferous hell.
With the few who overstep
Death's precipice,
I hold fast to the cocoon;
In Death's womb,
Consecrated by the soul's black fire,
I wait.
I bear the night's anguished wound,
For I know
As all children of the phoenix know,
This is not my first death
Nor will it be my last.
From fire I came, from fire I will go.
With each descent I will ascend
From my bed of ashes
Toward a triumphant heaven
With wings,
With wings,
With wings.

Visitation

In the barren desert of our days,
You may pass a prism garden
Lush with the light of a quiet soul
And you will know she has been there.
In the dark yearning of our years,
You may find a bountiful table
Overflowing with the abundance
Of an honest heart,
And you will know she has been there.
In the thorned dance to our destinations,
You may hear the haunting music
Of a bird,
And breathless, you will pause to listen,
And you will know she has been there,
An angel among us.

Blue Infinity

I do not know
If I am dancing this dream
Or dreaming the dance.
Days are flowers
Trembling against joy's illumined breast;
Nights, the silver wings of angels
Ascending into the storm's
Breathless fury.
Every step spins my soul
Into blue infinity.
As long as we have dreamt of Love,
Love has dreamt of us.

Spared

A weeping loon
Sends her prayer upon the waves
And listens for her echo to return
Upon the hour's dark wind.
It is the only thing that returns,
The only portion of her soul
Time or thief has not yet taken-
Her song in the starless nights.

Dark Night of the Soul

We search to find the phoenix,
A single feather from its burning flight,
Proof there is something of ourselves
Left to burn, to give light.
Dreams that remain are crimson leaves;
Two, three, no more, cling to November.
Our own lives, like trees in the twilight,
Though, entranced by forgetfulness,
Must put forth a solitary branch,
A single,
Faithful twig
That hopes for spring,
Hopes for all the others
Slumbering in darkness
On nights like this.

Provenance

Leaves pressed into a book
Mark a forgotten day,
Significance lost in a torrent of years.
Now impervious to season, far from limb,
Do they remember
The busy metropolis of roots
Or the galaxy of spring buds...
Can they recite the mute history of bark?
Do they remember their sire,
The towering bard
Who put words to the wind...
Do their souls return as birds,
Spilling harmony into the dawn?

Hotel Lobby

One hundred people
Pushing
Waiting
Passing
Shoulder-to-shoulder isolation
Each his own continent
With no connecting flights

Flames of the Stars

Metamorphosis

I have seen the flames of the stars
Flicker in the wind.
Like them, I embraced the night
When day threw her stones.
...And I have walked with Magdalene.

I have stood on foggy shores
With rebellion in the whitened waves
And in my hands.
I denied shelter when my nets
came up empty.
...And I have walked with Simon.

I have doubted
The most brilliant of miracles
And mocked the visions of other men.
...And I have walked with Thomas.

I have been tempted by gold and the
Silver of the earth.
I have betrayed and writhed in despair.
...I have walked with Judas.

Master Key

There are no lifetimes of happiness,
Only moments.

There are no destinations,
Only resting places.

There are no changes,
Only seasons.

Bridegroom

When the door between worlds
Is left ajar,
You come to me in the night
And burn above me
With shining wings
Of infinity
And a whisper inaudible
To the irreverent day.
Night Angel,
Lover of the storm's beating heart,
Husband of the Heavens,
Bridegroom of my soul,
I have forsaken lifetimes of constancy
For one elusive touch
That is no longer mine at dawn's coming.
Let me brave the thunder
Beneath your wings,
Beloved, eclipse the sun once more,
Once more.

The Bather

He swims in a platinum river,
Enveloped by the tides.
Are you man or god,
Strong as the stones
At the river's heart,
Soft and shimmering as rain,
Gold and alabaster
Carved by the silver fingers of the waters?
From this bluff, I cannot see your eyes,
Yet I know they are deep
And the color of the river's thoughts
And rapids are not half as wild
As your soul.
...Dancing, dissolving...
Tonight, in dreams, I will be silver water.

Eurydice

What is left to startle my soul
Now that I have tasted you?
What beauty, what burning,
What exquisite pain
Could ever suffice again?
In the deaf storm of my life,
Orpheus, I have heard your song;
Now I can live.
Into the deep sleep of hell,
You have followed my desire
To lead me from the abyss...
I know how the myth ended before,
Before I tasted you.
Please, this time, do not turn.
Do not turn to look behind.
Leave doubt in the depths.
Let me taste the sunlight.

Elegy for a Self

Her heart was a cup of sky;
One sip and you could taste
The storm over the mountains.
Her hand was a chisel
Against the defiant marble of dreams,
And her soul, a gossamer morning
Flung over the night.

She did not know the fragility
Of the goblet
Or the ravenous thirst;
The cold reality within the stone
Or the sword within the darkness.

Close her eyes;
Let the twilight take her.
Let her sisters sing the moon
Over her memory.
Cover her with disheveled night
And the leaves that blow
In the face of the storm.
Let fire bury fire.

Heather

Across the heather-embroidered moor,
A spirit walks...
Be cautious, my child,
When you hear her skirts
Billowing in the wind.
Some say she is a fay
Who weeps beneath the moon.
Others say she is a poet
Who has come back with unbraided hair
To find verses she has left behind.

Signature

Listening to the haiku
Of whispering waters,
Weeping pine boughs lean
To drink from reflection.

The pewter-wash of the lake's expanse
Fades into mist, into memory,
And the dreamer, tracing the shore,
Searches for the artist's lost signature.

Soul's Remembrance

The snow-tired heart
Awakens to spring,
And the night offers incense
Of thawing earth and April rain.
It is then
The soul will hear the litany of the winds
And look above its own greatness
To the stars and know which ones
Are the lanterns of the gods.

Resurrection

Cocooned in the dawn's gilded shroud,
I cast my heart's tattered remnant
Into the unknown.
A morning moon gathers her silver net
From an ebbing sea
While straight and unfaltering
As an arrow, I leave
The impoverished safety of the bow;
Unconquered in triumph's ascent,
I soar into the eagle's ecstasy...
All around me, scattering, falling,
The golden dust of outgrown dreams,
Yellow roses thrown
From the hands of the rising sun.

Sun on Water

Love Song to India

Once, I looked into the dark fire
Of your eyes
And danced in your perfumed temples
Garlanded with flowers
To your painted gods of gold.
From a dais of silk,
I kissed your impoverished hands
And envied the faceless grace
Of an untouchable
Walking your streets of dust.
I drank until intoxication
On your quest for beauty
And worshipped until nirvana
The raga of your broken soul.
I tasted your kiss in your cardamom
And inhaled eternity
From your sandalwood pyre.
I saw your mother's smile
Mirrored in the Ganges.
Once, I lived and died
In your ancient arms;
Though, transformed and veiled by time,
I have never forgotten you,
Barefoot, bejeweled, dark-eyed India.

Castaway

Outside, new moon dissolved by rain
Inside, these four walls
Island, no way off
Infinity of days
Waiting for this fire to be seen
Hope long dead
Dead as the last grains of incense
Burned hours ago
Sweetness barely lingering
In bitter memory

Escape

I waded through the meadow's
Wind-braided hair,
Scented grass to my knee,
And climbed the summit
And mocked the distant
Earthbound silhouettes
Against the billowing blue cape
Of twilight.
Great waves of wind
Bathed the wounds of the soul
Until it was no longer I
Who stood on the hill's patina brow
But a shining seraph
Catching the first star's silver
On my wings.
And far away...
Mingling with the muffled voices
Of approaching night,
The soft, crackling gallop
Of a mare through dry grass,
And on her wind-saddled back,
A girl singing toward home.

Biography in Driftwood

In a season of fury,
A storm ripped out a tree's soft heart
And set it adrift
Upon a ceaseless world of water.
Driftwood, hewn by
Fingers of circumstance
And seasoned against hearts of stone
Until you were impervious
To the rage of nights.
Burnished, sea-gray veteran,
How long the journey
To this vast, virgin shore;
Infinite hours proceeding toward
God
Beloved
Self
Finding all of them,
None of them.
Elusive trinity, ever present, ever unseen
In the transience of the tides,
The constancy of the swells.
Driftwood, refugee of the storm
Lost child of the forest,
Half-hewn creature of the sea...
Soft heart made wise and beautiful
In the harsh, exquisite womb
Of the waters.
A survivor of remembrance, this wood,

Polished and all too human;
A life like mine
That lends its voice to the Inaudible.
What we are, the wave has made.

Prayer by Prayer

Days die on the bough,
Untasted, uneaten, longed-for
With a hunger that rages.

(When did the mornings
Lose their sacredness?)

Age of the soul, not the body,
Tarnishes sunlight like forgotten silver.
A thief without a face
Pulled youth up like a weed
And crushed her temples
Prayer by prayer into silence.

(When did the mornings
Lose their sacredness?)

For Spring to Come...

Autumn...
And the forest has drunk its cup of time
Only to drink again from Rebirth.
Roots...
Limbs...
Drifting leaves...
Oh, rain-wept tree,
Unclothed ladder of the seasons,
Sleep.
Dream.
For spring to come,
Death must come first.

With the Wind's Turning

I thought I saw you,
Barely touched by the years.
Three steps behind you,
In the deafening crowd,
I thought I saw you.
The heart lives many lives then forgets.
Would you have known me
Beneath this painted mask of time?
Would your heart have remembered,
If only for a second,
Like a jewel of sun on water
That glimmers and glints
And then is gone
With the wind's turning?

Dusk

Sleep, dreaming of the dead
Dusk, threshold of storm
Leaves flying in ghost-wind
Ashes, embers drifting
The living, the dead-
Neither are free
Embers burning me
With wisdom
Dream of my father
Wearing his plaid shirt
Sitting at the table, weeping
Sleeping
Caught between worlds
Crying for the dead
And the dead crying for the living

Chasm

Chasm between ecstasy
And the sobriety of reason
Pause between the spaces of Now

When the music ceases
And the flaws of the dancer are seen
When hunger learns the difference
Between the crumbs and the feast
And the value of the least
Can no longer satiate
Pray to bear the pauses
And their weight

All Saint's Day

October's end
Fire of leaves smoldering
In the ash of cold rain
Dark water holding the memory of light
At a restless hour when all things
Murmur the reluctance of change

First Breath

Who I am

For you who never asked who I am
I am a blade turned on itself
Too unwilling to draw blood
For you who never asked who I am
I have a name
And a heart wasted in vain
I gave a soul
And a thousand selves
To mend you whole
For you who never asked who I am
I have a voice
In this silent war
I am not your whore
Or your stepping stone
For you who never asked who I am
I am a storm you cannot see
Gathering wind
Gathering speed
For you who never asked who I am
I am a force
You will reckon with
A source
You underestimated
Desecrated
Dismissed with careless hand
To answer what you never asked
This is who I am

Ashore

Night folds a velvet wing
Over darkening waters.
Compliant waves, undeterred by rock,
Swirl into sleep.
A life spared from the deep
Rests on the shore,
Waiting for slumber too still for dreams.

Emergence

Night of metamorphosis
Out of the chrysalis
Eons of winter obliterated
Out of the abyss
Out of the cocoon toward noon
Into light
And bright beauty
Wings tired from birth
Wings not of this earth

Initiate

Through the underworld of self
He travels the night shore,
Aware of the black wave
Cresting in silence.
Remembering the succulent kiss of sun,
He glances backward once more
Then turns to face
The nocturnal teacher.

Persephone

Your smile is carved from sunlight
As you happen to pass through my
Darkness.
You are a butterfly streaming light,
Yet you brave my heart's net of shadows.
Before you depart on the wind,
Teach me about transience,
Speak of wings;
Remind me
I, too, am a child of the cocoon.

First Breath

I left my crutch of pain
At the water's edge;
I unfurled my wings
In the blind, summer dusk,
And my veil of sleep blew away...
I emptied my cup of tears
In Love's great expanse
And drank laughter's wine.
The faiths I had lost
Washed in with the night.
I cleaned the stains from childhood's lace
And mended the tatters of broken smiles.
I opened the door to my Inner quiet,
And my splintered selves came home.
Tonight,
I hold the unfaltering flame of Self,
And as the sea leaves
Bracelets of foam around my ankles,
I take my first breath of Now.

Parole

Out of darkness
Into chaos of sun and sound
Dress, speak, continue on
Scared for eye to meet eye
Scared the world can see this soul
Still soiled from hell

Dress, speak, continue on
As if these shoulders
Never carried the burden of self

Yes, I have murdered
I have stolen
I have shattered
My own dreams
My own potential
My own innocence

Dress, speak, continue on
Terrified to trust
This scarred freedom

Haiku

September undresses the myrtle;
Fuchsia river of blossoms
And fierce tears.
Beneath a painted umbrella,
I walk, invisible
Against the day's gray heart,
Footsteps reciting the poetry
Of torn flowers.

Plenty

Spring tree just reborn
Reaching into heaven with full hands
Gestation of snow, womb of buds
Peridot hour of jeweled innocence
Solitary reveler walking on shadows
Spring heart reborn
Reaching into heaven with full hands

Envy

Purple crocus, already dead
Beneath March snow.
A hopeful friend,
She smiled for only a day or two
And promised to return next year.
The birds are home again,
And their song closes the day.
Happy singers, the sky is threatening
Yet still you sing...

From a Distant Window

Spell

Wisteria moon intoxicated with light
Night, drunk on awakening
May, eager and undaunted
As the epiphany of a smile
That leaves the heart stunned
Love in solitary dance
In dervish-spin
Ecstasy as futile
As a snowflake in the sun
Blossomed youth, an honored guest
Sups on unattainable dreams
Too beautiful to die in vain
Too soon sober
The world will return to itself
Reason disoriented as a moth in daylight

1967

Sunlight shines through a memory;
A dancing child with summer in her hair
When the air smelled like rain and youth
And the world raged beyond
The perimeter of our dreams.
Sunlight shines through a memory;
An artist on the street
With blue eyes like a sleeping sea
And my skirt that made you think
Of Gypsies...
We danced and drank the hour.
We knew we were only leaves,
Thoughts lost on the winds,
Memories shining through the sunlight
Of a distant day.

Centuries

Indigo tapestry of sky
Embroidered with stars
Centuries of burning
Canopied over our insignificance
Eyes heavenward
Infinite hunger for the Unattainable

The Star

With a net to catch the stars,
I ran through the night.
A daughter of the earth,
I reached far beyond my gaze
To a star holding the west with quiet light
And dreams of my childhood days.

Through starry fields,
I roamed without roots, without wings,
And you dared to shine
Greater than the moon.
You left your trusted throne,
Night's ancient king,
And followed me to youth's blazing noon.

But I peered into my net
When the journey was done
And found only dried leaves of despair.
Beyond my ladder of hope
And your stairway of time,
I was here...and you still there,
Despite my heart's undaunted climb.

Passages

The moon is a bronze flower
Wilting and waning in the east.
Suspended in silence
Between night and dawn.
Unseduced by sleep, I, too,
Am suspended in the night...
Somewhere
Between birth's maternal breast
And death's inevitable embrace.
An old dream limps in the wind
And settles in a temporary doorway
Of hope.
As a homeless man,
Hungry, forgotten.
My eyes remain sober
As my kin, my lover, and my friend
Sleep somewhere
Beneath the night's star-stitched blanket.
But for me, there is no bed prepared.
Destiny has eluded me.
I consult the Sybil, the old gypsy moon
And her near-death eyes.
There are no perpetual dwellings,
Only doorways...
We are only guests
Beneath her withered smile.

Dawn, like a red-haired woman,

Arches her body across the east,
Her womb a passage for the sun
And sleep for tired eyes.

Letter to the Soul

You have found no reflection
In the waters,
No mirror in man...
Yet, you have been
A flower's sweet song of fragrance
And circles of rain
In a storm-blackened pond.

You have conquered
The swift current of years,
Impervious to the transgressions of time.
Who am I to question the path
You have hewn for me?
I am but another costume
You have chosen
For Destiny's masquerade,
A needy child,
An embryo of experience
Beside your ancient divinity.

In the hollow heart of nights,
I have seen a flicker of fire
Through this maze of pain...
Has it been you, listening
From a distant window,
Though, my darkness has tried
To burn the beauty from your existence?

How many times I have abandoned you
By the bitter wayside
Only to find that you've gently
Limped your way home once again...
How many times I have mistaken
A demon's eyes for your shelter...
How many times I have forsaken you,
Soul of mine,
Soul Divine?

I am stripped of rebellion,
And all of your truths, I forgive.
Can you hear me, Soul of mine,
Soul Divine?
I want to live. I want to live.

This consciousness is but a facet
Within your great prism
Searching for a sunbeam
To ignite my memory of you.

Lady April

The world is on the threshold of blooming
As April returns from her wandering.
Where does she go
While the soul sleeps beneath the snows,
And how does she know
When the first robin
Jewels the twilight with singing,
Ringing in pale, gold days?
Lady April, back from her wandering,
Wears a single crocus in her hair...
Incense of earth offered to the winds
And the heart, again a new canvas,
Shivers beneath the touch of sable.
Heart on the precipice of blooming,
With no knowledge of snows,
This flower has only one thought,
One thought...
And that is to bloom
For the sake of blooming.

Evolution

I bury tired dreams
As the sun shuts its eyes
Over the mountain's breast.
Though, sun, you were brief
And dreams, you were few,
You will forget me in your timeless rest,
But I will remember you.
Night folds her sapphire arms
Across the day;
I sit beneath the stars,
Wise, brokenhearted, but free.
Dreams, I watch you dance away.
Remember me.

Kindred

We were severed when the Circle began
And then severed again.
We were scattered by the winds
And thrown into Time.
We said goodbye
In the tunnel to the womb
Knowing we would always share
The same blood
And the only home we would ever find
Is in each other's eyes.
Soul Sister
Soul Brother,
I see you in the stars
And hear your voice in the sea.
You are unknown,
But I think of you
When I walk against the wind,
Knowing somewhere,
You walk a road leading into mine.

Source

We consume fruit and flesh
Of the fields;
Are we not earth?
Beneath bodily soil,
Our spirits are of the wind;
Are we not air?
Impassioned, we dance
To the heart;
We burn...Love, our fuel;
Are we not fire?
Over waves of laughter
And rocks of turmoil,
We flow urgently toward the Destination;
Are we not water?

Marlaina Donato

When the Night
Rains Memories

poems

When the Night

Rains Memories

Bitter Brine

The Chase

Run 'til the heart is bloodless and the lungs breathless,

Until the sweat of the chase exhausts.

Through flowered fields (no time to drink beauty)

Through succulent glens (no time to taste the fruit)

Day after day, year after year, age after age,

The hunter and the hunted.

Self

Soul of sapphire and bitter brine,

Wring out the sea that bore you;

Cast off the thirst never quelled;

Turn inland to the desert

Where desire dies in the sands

And stands more beautiful in death,

Blanched and gleaming, whiter than sea-foam.

Turn toward Home, Soul of spindrift

Where fire will teach you barrenness,

Where demons will make you unbreakable;

Soul of sapphire and brine, become desert wind,

Free of desire, soul of fire.

Woman

My father is the sun,

My mother the rain.

I

Did

Not

Bloom

For

You,

For you to pull out petals

Into your fist.

If I mirror beauty,

It is beauty not intended

To entertain your evil.

I

Did

Not

Bloom

For

You,

For you to rape my soul

With your words or your eyes.

This is why the serpent has venom,

The lioness her rage,

And the rose its thorn.

I hope you bleed well.

Aeternus

Moon, you dance on the waters,

Emptied of youth

And bearing the burden of centuries;

You will dance infinitely

Until your last quiver of light

After we have ceased to dance.

Midsummer's Night

The night is a lonely painter,

And we talk as I sit in the garden.

Twilight is still wet

When he brushes in the stars.

Fireflies explode against the canvas

As we watch your silhouette

Inside the door,

Your hands a blur of conversation

Against bronze light.

He tells me that he was young once,

And I tell him

I could watch you for hours,

Your hair windblown from the day.

I tell him I love you,

And he paints the moon's smile.

One

Branches dripping October rain

Weeping wood and dying flames of leaves

Return to the old path

Search for squandered summers

No remnant here

(Season and soul are tired)

Too late to breathe

A wandering wind sweet with wild grape

Vines sleeping in the wet

Harvest accomplished, purpose fulfilled

Too late to gather

Save for the one remaining

Wild grape on the tongue

Sweet leaning toward bitter

Like all tired things

Requiem

...No light tonight,

No blaze of moon or wick of star,

Only the rain's cool mantra, hour upon hour.

Twenty seasons ago tonight,

A quiet soul left in the rain;

Each year, in soft weeping,

The clouds remember.

The Artist

Even in darkness you will not see him holding a candle
flame;

Though his pen and palette sow your world with visions,

You will not remember his name.

In your hour of laughter,

You will be blind to his abyss of tears.

Your oblivious step will seek the dance;

Though his song drifts by, you will never hear.

Your fear will mock his arrows aimed at beauty's quest,

Yet you will envy his hunger for the unembraceable

And count the sins within the robe his soul is dressed.

You will cling to the hearth when winter scars the pane,

And your children will dream by the fire

As his rootless shadow weds the rain.

If for a moment you know him,

You will only know him

For his madness born from ideals, broken-winged.

Weathered, in a shroud of bitterness,

He leaves this world neither pauper nor king.

Only then will you know

The candle that illumined the night,

And another generation

Will claim his legacy of light.

Chosen

Night pulls me to you;

My heart burns through the darkness,

A meteor bound for your desire;

Unquenchable, unyielding

Blazing into death- or rebirth,

While you wait with open palm

In the silent calm

Of knowing.

We are the chosen,

Not the choice.

Witness

Smoke drifts into the night, no one is scarcely aware;

The home that once stood in afternoon shade,

A cloak of tired ember wears;

But through the canopy of smoke,

Stars hold their light.

And upon the staircase,

Burned and broken,

The ancient, new moon shines tonight.

Blood in Bloom

Roses in the Snow

There is a generation

That walks a razor's edge

Of sadness and celebration,

A generation

From cut-down family trees,

Black and blue lives and addiction's disease;

A generation growing in the cold

In the divorce depot and runaway station,

A generation too late heard, too soon old

But in the cold

They grow

Like roses in the snow.

Through the Eyes of Timmy

through the curtain, i watch them leave

now i can go out and play

(i'm not a bad boy but they never listen)

my face ripples in the rain

and i make believe the air is my castle

and the puddle is my moat

go away, mister, don't ask about my shoulder

or my eye

(hurry, they're coming down the road, don't cry)

I hope they see my castle in the driveway

(hurry, don't cry)

It has walls as tall as the sky

(hurry, don't cry)

only the rain can cry

Rekindled

Lantern of winter moon

And inside, this fragile fire

Long hours against you

Long rivers of our laughter

Long tears

Long regret

For the heart's wasted years

Lantern of winter moon

And inside, this fragile fire

Long hours against you

Long tears

Long promises

For the heart's coming years

Certainty

We share an apple,

And you make me laugh,

A gallery of faces and your little boy smile.

How I wish we had been children together,

Vagabonds in stained denim,

Stories tangling our hair.

I would have chosen you across the room,

Your blue-eyed sadness;

I would have heard your soul,

Its mischief and its longing,

Known you without a word as I know you now.

"You never grew up," I say, smoothing the gray

In your mustache, loving you loving me.

"It all started with an apple," you say,

Offering me another bite of October.

We will finish the apple and spend

The afternoon with Kerouac and Kipling,

Miller and Whitman,

And then find our bed beneath a waning moon

And an exodus of clouds.

Spooned in whisper and hunger,

We will ride the wave to stillness,

And like a stone

On the river's dark bed of centuries,

I will know the certainty of your arms

Beneath changing rapids.

Velvet

Dry harvest in the poverty of rains

Tilling the days

Pulling up weeds of regret

Sudden petals

A single flower

Barren plain startled by crimson

Fragrance as deep as velvet

From what hand, what seed

Were you born

I do not remember

Sowing this blood in bloom

This flower the color of heart's precipice

And August storm

Pluck the velvet from the dirt

And run, face uplifted toward heaven

Petals blowing

Spilling red rain into the wind

Honeysuckle

The taste of cold water

And this afternoon

In the palm of May

I taste the bread of us

Hearts beating honeysuckle

Wild geranium beneath our steps

We feast on spring

That will not come again

White Linen

Morning broken on your steps

Pieces of light and your mosaic table

Chiffon of leaves over the door

A counter busy with books

And papers and days

the scent of ginger

Blue twist of stair

A bed white with dreams

Stray heart passing through

Soiled and dreaming

Of linen, clean and new

Burial

Hope gutted

Heart sacrificed

Night of blood

Love, stillborn in the dawn

Yes, you were love

And you had a name

You had a name

Night Thunder

A pulse in the darkness

Music on the pier, drums on the beach

Night of youth, thunder

Hunger

In the blood

Poetry in the waves

Wind in the wilds of your hair

Dance

Chance

Morning will be hollow...again

Tomorrow

Will make us old,

My borrowed friend

Pain sleeps on the deep

Forget how to weep

Night of youth, thunder,

Hunger

In the blood

Before dawn returns with age

Before Fate turns the page

And destiny dies

Memorize

This bliss

This kiss

Of fevered flight

On broken wings

Futility sings,

"Never forget or regret…"

The Idol

Upon desolate sand, I knelt with tired feet

At the base of a sculpture of gold.

Beneath the burning sun,

I held out my hand

And offered my soul.

A humble believer, I bowed

To the god with painted eyes

And worshipped its glory

Beaming in the sun,

'Til the blazing ember cooled

And left the skies,

'Til the arid day was done.

But when I stood

And shadows fell with night,

The idol that in the afternoon shone,

Lost its cloak of sunset light

And was not god, not gold...but stone.

Second Wind

Unforeseen

Alighting in your doorway,

I sought shelter from the tempest.

How safe you were

While the world drowned;

A safe, warm hand.

The door slammed.

The storm died long, long ago.

Too tired to fight,

I remember the taste of dawn

And the wind on my wings.

"Let me out..." no longer youth's desperate scream,

But a whisper so faint it is a prayer.

Morning Honey

Your cup with the painted leaves

Your profile against a window

And wet light on your words

Wishing I was the sun

Through the yellow curtain

Dripping day onto your smile

Scars

"It's been a long day," you said

And went to bed

Every night the same

Your life's flame

At wick's end

Soul tired with ages

Beneath the weight of scars

You never looked at stars

With me again

Years since you flickered out

My youth since weathered

Soul tired with ages

Beneath the weight of scars

I look at stars

Tonight to find your face

Faith, friend, and fire all burned away

I pray for a longer wick

Daddy, it's been a long, long day

Second Wind

In the shadow of spinning wheels,

A girl pauses on a rose-pink bike,

Her smile, a blue-eyed April.

Child of ten summers

And hair blowing light,

Your soul has yet to bear

The weight of bitter winter.

You are a pale, sweet flower

To a heart grown gray

With too many Decembers.

I watch your spinning wheels

Disappear into the distance,

The sun descending at your back.

Perhaps, someday, when your heart has seen

Too many snows,

You will glimpse April in a child's face

And sow again.

Apartment 41

Unseen, summer slips away

As quietly as the woman

Who took her life.

Cornflowers still color the walkway,

Oblivious to the footsteps

That will never touch this concrete again.

Bells still haunt the twilight

From the steeple at the end of the street,

Though she will not hear their voices

From her window two flights up.

The shoemaker still closes on Tuesdays,

And the kids in Apartment 44

Still leave their bikes

Overturned on the sidewalk

Across from the church

With the red doors.

Amber lights still pierce

The ten o'clock fog,

And a brass lamp still remains lit

In the office below the sealed apartment.

Only the dead know what has changed.

Ashes

During an hour of thirst,

I looked to you for water;

I did not know you were a desert.

During an hour of exile

I looked for a beating heart;

I did not know you were a stone.

During an hour of dying

I searched for a soul;

I forgot I had my own.

During an hour of blindness,

I gave you light.

During an hour of snow,

I gave you warmth.

How long can a fire burn?

Quests

Breakers bubbled into foam

As we looked for shells.

On a gray morning, we left our prints

In the mirror-sand.

Clam, oyster, angel's wing

Filled my childhood pail,

Yet remained bare of our quest: sea glass.

You spoke of other shores

As I kept my eyes to the beach.

We stole the treasures that had

Washed in with the night-

Pebbles of quartz, lost pennies,

Sand dollars.

"Maybe tomorrow morning," you said,

Just as I looked down one last time.

There, in the net of my gaze,

I snared a piece of broken bottle,

Polished and tossed by the sea.

Nothing remains

From that morning walk,

Except our quest-

Wrapped in the unspoken.

And in a treasure box- sea glass.

Uncompensated

The heart is a wounded soldier

Barefoot through Hell too long

(Do we ever return home?)

We carry the abyss forever

With no visible scars

No reward for surviving

Veterans of ourselves

Bouquet

You smile, opening the door

After our first argument

A profusion of roses, apology in white

Felicity

Pressed Flower

Between forgotten pages

A rose, plucked

From the warm hand of summer,

Is safe from the season's turning.

In its shroud of silence,

Does it remember its scarlet hour

Or the want of rain?

Has it forgotten

The child's button nose

Nestled in its fragrance

One a lost June day?

All the others withered

In the battle to hold the sun;

Only one was spared

To be the others' memory

Diamonds

Last Memory

Pouring rain, a thousand fairy drums

Under an umbrella, just you and me

In the circle of your arm

Your hand traveling the length

Of my spine in slow waves

Amber lights staining the road

I will remember this

When I am dying

I will fly

On the wings of this memory

Of the warmth of your soul against me

With the night raining down

Cross my Heart

On a deserted playground

You asked me not to tell.

"Cross my heart, hope to die."

With your red ponytail

Blowing in the breeze

You told me what he did,

About the hands in the night.

Promise you won't tell?

"Cross my heart, hope to die."

The merry-go-round unwound to a stop.

I called you a liar.

Today, our six-year-old voices

Drift back.

If only I could

Break my promise

And tell the world about what he did,

About the hands in the night.

Too little, too late,

"I'm sorry..." borrowed child of the breeze.

"Cross my heart, hope to die."

Quenched

Summer shakes out her apron of shadows;

In a lap of shade, we taste cherries warmed by a lover's hand.

As the morning billows like wind-fresh linen,

In the cool cascade of your arms,

I drink forever.

Nightfall

Fears dart into a tired brain

Like bats into darkness.

I lie against the earth,

Aching for laughter

As seeds ache for the wind.

And in a night overflowing with voices,

We cry.

We cry inaudibly.

Diamonds

Night bridge

Strung with diamond light

Jewel-stained breast of river

Shimmering until dawn

Out of the womb of darkness,

Scarlet sun

One by one, bridge lights put to bed

Diamonds into a velvet pouch

Water, naked and unadorned

Sober by day

The Apple

Autumn fragranced the air

As we gathered apples after the rain.

The late shower baptized

Their sweet, crimson cheeks,

And high over my head,

My young hands strained

To grasp the fruit

Ripened that last sunny week.

Below her twisted trunk,

Her children colored the ground.

But the best and sweetest

Were still embraced by the bough.

And though there were plenty

Scattered 'round,

My heart was set on one

High above my brow.

Seeing my despair,

With your needed height and concern,

You did understand...

Plucking the gem with gentle might,

You placed the shining, red sphere

In my hand.

Autumn Fires

Summer withers

In the tree's blush of dying

Heart remembering

When you illumined the world

Before your breath went out

Autumn was flame then, fire blazing

Not a slipping-away

The world wearing your death

As I go on living

Silver Birds

The moon of summer's end

Waxes toward midnight

Sending shadows into the lap of the lawn;

Her silver birds of light descending

Beneath the sycamore.

A swing, uninspired by the breeze,

Waits for the child, now grown, to return.

Tired leaves scurry

Across all roads not taken,

And night drops her curtain

Heaviest on the pathway chosen.

Unfinished Canvas

For twenty summers

You watched the color of my eyes

Blend into yours

And my profile become your cameo.

But it was that autumn

I became your daughter.

Did you know I memorized your words

As we circled the pond?

Did you know my youth would be

Defined beneath your orchards,

Or my soul reborn

Upon the dais of your easel?

Now, thirty summers, thirty pages turned,

And our book finished, closed.

I remember my portrait

Half-painted,

Deprived of your signature,

And the nights and dreams

I left in my father's studio.

Infinity

Dawn, a seed of light pushes

Through the dark soil of nights;

Breathless, deathless, she goes on.

Through the timeless mantra of mornings,

The sun's perennial ambition shames the stars;

Breathless, deathless, he goes on.

Through the abyss to the summit

And through the abyss again,

Breathless, deathless, we go on.

Broken Goblet

Glimmer

Your name once a holy invocation

Is now a word as ordinary as any other,

One rarely used or remembered,

Its meaning now cold, save for a passing

Flicker of fire on the tongue.

Noon

Light on linen, white shoulders in the sun

Ivory curtains blowing shadows across your bareness

Orange, half-peeled and dripping gold

In the white of the day

For my Mother

When we are gone they will find our ghosts here,

Here among the trees amid this russet light.

Someday, a child will glimpse

Your smile in the sun

And hear your voice and my guitar in the wind.

Song of my song, soul of my soul,

We will be the story they tell

When the night rains memories.

Disillusionment

Clinging shadow, tripping my steps

Like Mother's gown when I was a child;

Side by side competing for a thing called love.

And like Mama's dress, I wanted to wear your lace

And walk in your shoes;

Oh, how I envied your lofty place.

Once, you were fine and new,

But that was another day,

And now, the dream still keeps me

From folding and putting your torn lace away.

Passage

As if hewn from shadow,

A silhouetted world upholds a dying sun.

The stenciled form of a man, a boat gliding through

Gold-washed waters amid blowing rice.

We stand at the edge of the day

In this ecstasy of light,

Hallowed, this passage into night.

The Vineyard

My hands cup rushing water,

And its sparkling dream escapes my fingers.

The horizon holds the sun's fire,

But the embers soon die.

Trying to catch a runaway child, frustration lingers.

I long to hold sweet-hearted spring

As I once hurried the winter;

Oh, I have outgrown this tarnished ring.

In a vintage of unripened fruit, I peer...

I seek vintage wine, my glass filled with dreams.

But Dionysos, you have not been here,

And beneath trodden dust, my broken goblet gleams.

Homecoming

Desire melts like spring

Summer in your body

Spared from snow, the flower of my life pressed against you

Soft fire surpassing the blazes of youth

Second April

Litha

This holy hour of Midsummer

Our spirits go barefoot

Imprinting prayers in the dust.

Mother of the ancient earth,

Lady of thunder, goddess of the turning tide,

You scent the night

With your breath of flowers

And the wet bark of your wild places.

Father of the cosmic sun,

Bringer of first fruits, lord of the tempest, our souls come
home to you,

Thirsty for the deep kiss of your rivers

And hungry for your harvest of truth.

We gather our scattered selves

And offer our hearts scarred from too many winters.

Opium

I miss myself before you

Miss my blood before it was yours

Miss desolate freedom and the virgin canvas

Before your signature in razor's edge

Before your eyes in the sun

And the spiral galaxies between your thighs

Before the monotony of your memory

Before consciousness

Bluebells

We waited beneath the dogwood tree

For the bus to take us to school.

We leaned our books against

Its twisted trunk and huddled

Beneath the pink umbrella of blossoms

In the sunless chill.

We counted the petals

That looked like valentines

And the bluebells on your dress.

Your name and love of counting

Dogwood hearts

Were the only things I knew about you,

And you knew no more of me.

Each day we would count

A few more than the day before.

From second grade to fourth,

We never counted them all

And never knew

If we counted a few twice.

You are forgotten as a stone

Thrown into a pool

Until the dogwood

Opens her blushing umbrella

Or I see spring linen

Dotted with bluebells.

Poetry is the golden child of observation and catharsis—or so it is for poet-author-artist Marlaina Donato. Her passion for words was sparked at age ten when her mother gave her a copy of Whitman's *Leaves of Grass*. Marlaina soon found her own Muse, scribbling onto bits of paper and in journals. Reading and writing poetry became necessity-bread for the soul and a compass to live by.

Marlaina Donato is the author of several books including *Spiritual Famine in the Age of Plenty* and the novel *Broken Jar*. She is also a professional artist. She and her beloved husband Joe live in beautiful rural New Jersey. To learn more about her books or to peruse

her online visual art galleries, please visit:
www.marlainadonato.com

Index to First Lines